Philip Ridley

Leaves of Glass

Methuen Drama

Published by Methuen Drama 2007

3 5 7 9 10 8 6 4 2

Methuen Drama
A & C Black Publishers Limited
38 Soho Square
London W1D 3HB
www.acblack.com

ISBN: 978 0 713 68858 0

A CIP catalogue record for this book
is available from the British Library

Typeset by Country Setting, Kingsdown, Kent
Printed and bound in Great Britain by
MPG Books Ltd, Bodmin, Cornwall

Caution

● soho theatre

Soho Theatre presents

Leaves of Glass

by Philip Ridley

First performed at Soho Theatre on 3 May 2007

Leaves of Glass is supported by the Harold Hyam Wingate Foundation, The Paul Hamlyn Foundation

Soho Theatre is supported by

Performances in the Lorenz Auditorium

Registered Charity No: 267234

Leaves of Glass

by Philip Ridley

Barry	**Trystan Gravelle**
Debbie	**Maxine Peake**
Liz	**Ruth Sheen**
Steven	**Ben Whishaw**

Director	**Lisa Goldman**
Designer	**Laura Hopkins**
Lighting	**Jenny Kagan**
Sound	**Matt McKenzie**
Fight Director	**Bret Young**

Production Manager	Matt Noddings
Stage Manager	Dani Youngman
Deputy Stage Manager	Emily Peake
Assistant Stage Manager	Natasha Emma Jones
Wardrobe Supervisor	Hilary Lewis
Head Technician	Nick Blount
Head of Lighting	Christoph Wagner
Lighting Technician	Mark Watts
Scenery built by	Revolving Stage Company
Press Representation	Nancy Poole (020 7478 0142)
Photography	Manuel Harlan

Soho Theatre, 21 Dean Street, London W1D 3NE
Admin: 020 7287 5060   Fax: 020 7287 5061
Box Office: 0870 429 6883
www.sohotheatre.com

Biographies

Writer

Philip Ridley *Writer*

Philip was born in the East End of London where he still lives and works. He studied painting at St Martin's School of Art and his work has been exhibited throughout Europe and Japan. As well as three books for adults – and the highly acclaimed screenplay for the *The Krays* feature film - he has written five other adult stage plays: *The Pitchfork Disney*, the multi-award-winning *The Fastest Clock in the Universe*, *Ghost from a Perfect Place*, *Vincent River*, and the highly controversial *Mercury Fur*, plus a further five plays for young people; *Karamazoo, Fairytaleheart, Moonfleece, Sparkleshark* and *Brokenville*. He has also directed two films from his own screenplays: *The Reflecting Skin* – winner of eleven international awards – and *The Passion of Darkly Noon* (winner of the Best Director Prize at the Porto Film Festival). Philip has also written many books for children including *Scribbleboy* (shortlisted for the Carnegie Medal), *Kasper in the Glitter* (nominated for the Whitbread Prize), *Mighty Fizz Chilla* (shortlisted for the Blue Peter Book of the Year Award), *ZinderZunder, Vinegar Street, Zip's Apollo* and *Krindlekrax* (winner of both the Smarties Prize and WH Smith's Mind-Boggling Books Award), the stage play of which – adapted by Philip himself – was premiered at the Birmingham Rep Theatre in the summer of 2002. Philip has won both the Evening Standard's Most Promising Newcomer to British Film and Most Promising Playwright Awards. The only person ever to receive both prizes.

Cast

Trystan Gravelle Barry

Theatre includes: *Days Of Significance, Winters Tale* (Nominated for The Ian Charleson Award), *Pericles, The Birthday Party, A Midsummer Night's Dream, As You Like It, Taming of the Shrew, Romeo And Juliet, Hamlet, Macbeth* (all at RSC). Films include: *A Way of Life.* Television includes: *Cardiff, A470, The Chosen* (Nominated for Best Newcomer, BAFTA Wales 2004).

Maxine Peake Debbie

Theatre includes: *On the Third Day* (New Ambassadors Theatre), *Rutherford & Son* (Royal Exchange), *Robin Hood* (RNT), *Serjeant Musgrave's Dance* (Oxford Stage Company), *Hamlet* (West Yorkshire Playhouse), *Mother Theresa Is Dead* (Royal Court), *Luther, The Relapse, The Cherry Orchard* (RNT), *Miss Julie* (Theatre Royal Haymarket), *Early One Morning*

(Bolton Octagon). Film includes: *Clubbed, All Or Nothing, Girls Night*. Television includes: *Confessions Of A Diary Secretary, See No Evil, Messiah, Faith, Shameless, Christmas Lights, Early Doors, The Way We Live Now, Victoria Wood & All The Trimmings, Dinner Ladies, Clocking Off, Hetty Wainthrop Investigates*.

Ruth Sheen   Liz

Theatre includes: *An Oak Tree* (Soho Theatre), *Market Boy* (RNT), *Stoning Mary* (Royal Court and Drum Theatre, Plymouth), *It's A Great Big Shame, Red Riding Hood* (Theatre Royal, Stratford East), *Dreamer, Children For Sale, Short Circuit* (Half Moon Theatre), *Crime Of The Century, Meg and Mog* (Wolsey Theatre), *Ten Tiny Fingers* (Library Theatre), *The Home Service* (Bloomsbury Theatre), *As You Like It* (Ludlow and tour), *Othello, Kept In/Kept Out*. Film includes: *Run Fat Boy Run, Vera Drake, Vanity Fair, Cheeky, All Or Nothing, Bait, Secrets And Lies, Virtual Sexuality, The Young Poisoner's Handbook, Little Dorrit, High Hopes* (European Actress Of The Year in 1989), *The Angry Earth*. Television includes: *The Spastic King, A Class Apart, Vital Signs, An English Harem, Doc Marten, Footprints In The Snow, Miss Marple, Plain Jane, Lorna Doone, Never Never, Don Quixote, Berkeley Square, Tom Jones, Cracker, Holding On, Bramwell, Sin Bin, Downtown Lagos, Clubland, A Fatal Inversion, Crossing The Border,* *London's Burning, The Bill, King And Castle, Making Out* and *Nightvoice*.

Ben Whishaw   Steven

Theatre includes: *The Seagull* (RNT), *Mercury Fur* (Paines Plough), *Hamlet* (Old Vic), *His Dark Materials* (RNT). Television includes: *Nathan Barley, Booze Cruise, Ready When You Are Mr McGill, Other People's Children*. Film includes: *I'm Not There, Perfume: The Story Of A Murderer, Stoned, Enduring Love,* 77 *Beds, Layer Cake, The Trench, My Brother Tom, The Escort*.

Company

Lisa Goldman   Director

Lisa is the new Artistic Director of Soho Theatre and *Leaves of Glass* by Philip Ridley is her first show in this role. As founding Artistic Director of the Red Room, Lisa developed and directed a huge body of radical new writing over 10 years. Her last production was *Hoxton Story*, a site-specific walkabout piece which she wrote and directed. Other recent new plays developed and directed include *The Bogus Woman* (Fringe First – Bush/Traverse/tour/Radio 3 Sunday play), *Bites* (Bush Theatre) and *Animal* (Soho Theatre), *Hanging* (CBL Radio 4 Friday play) all by Kay Adshead, curating *Going Public* (Tricycle Theatre), *Playing Fields* by Neela Dolezalova (Soho Theatre Company), *Made in England* by Parv Bancil, *Sunspots, Know*

Your Rights and *People on the River* all by Judy Upton. *Ex, Obsession* and *Surfing* (Critics' Choice BAC) and a 35mm short film *My Sky is Big* (NFT 1 & festivals) all by Rob Young. Lisa's long term producing collaboration with Anthony Neilson has enabled the creation of some of his finest work - *The Censor, Stitching* (both Time Out Live Award winners) and *The Night Before Christmas.* In 2001 Lisa co-founded Artists Against the War.

Laura Hopkins   Designer

Laura trained at Motley. Her design work includes: *Black Watch* (National Theatre of Scotland), *Sinatra!* (costumes), *Mercury Fur* (Paines Plough), *The Three Musketeers* (Bristol Old Vic), *Hotel Methuselah* (Imitating The Dog), *The Escapologist* (suspect Culture), *Jerusalem and Mr Heracles* (TMA winner Best Design) (Both West Yorkshire Playhouse), *Under The Black Flag, The Storm, Dido, Queen of Carthage, The Golden Ass* and *Macbeth* (all at Shakespeare's Globe), *Cosi Fan Tutte* and *Falstaff* (both ENO), *Hamlet, Faustus* (TMA winner, Best Design) and *Othello* (also nominated for TMA award (all Northampton Royal), *The INS Broadcasting Unit* (ICA), *Elixir of Love* (New Zealand Opera), *Swan Lake Re-mixed* (Vienna Volksoper), Carnesky's *Ghost Train* (a visual theatre ride), *Claire de Luz, Blood* and *If We Shadows* (all Insomniac productions with Pete Brooks).

Jenny Kagan   Lighting Designer

Jenny trained as an actress and worked as a stage manager before turning to lighting design. Productions include: *Pan* (Capitol Theatre Sydney), *Sacred Ellington* performed by Jessye Norman (Barbican Centre), *Who's Afraid Of Virginia Woolf* (Almeida and Aldwych Theatre), *Oliver!* (Australian, US and UK Tours), *Elisir d'Amour* (New Zealand Festival) and the recent UK tour of *Miss Saigon.* She worked with David Hersey on *Piaf, The Seagull, Martin Guerre, Jesus Christ Superstar, Les Misérables* (UK tour, Sydney, Antwerp and Dublin). She was Associate Lighting Designer for *Oklahoma* (RNT, West End, Broadway & Primetime Films) and has also worked on shows at The Bush, Tricycle, West Yorkshire Playhouse and Edinburgh Lyceum. Recently she worked with Lisa Goldman on *The Hoxton Story* for the Red Room and *Bites* (Bush Theatre).

Matt McKenzie   Sound Designer

Matt McKenzie came to the UK from New Zealand in 1978. He toured with Paines Plough before joining the staff at The Lyric Theatre Hammersmith in 1979 where he designed the sound for several productions. Since joining Autograph in 1984, Matt has been responsible for the sound design for the opening of Soho Theatre along with its production of *Blue Eyes and Heels, Badnuff, Vertigo* (Guildford), *Saturday, Sunday,*

Monday, Easy Virtue (Chichester), *Frame 312* (Donmar Warehouse), *Iron* (The Traverse and Royal Court). In the West End, theatre credits include: *Made in Bangkok, The House of Bernarda Alba, A Piece of My Mind, Journey's End, A Madhouse in Goa, Barnaby and the Old Boys, Irma Vep, Gasping, Map of the Heart, Tango Argentino, When She Danced, Misery, Murder is Easy, The Odd Couple, Pygmailion, Things we do for Love, Long Day's Journey into Night* and *Macbeth*. For Sir Peter Hall credits include: *Lysistrata, The Master Builder, School for Wives, Mind Millie for Me, A Streetcar Named Desire, Three of a Kind* and *Amedeus* (West End and Broadway). Matt was Sound Supervisor for the Peter Hall Season (Old Vic and The Piccadilly) and designed the sound for *Waste, Cloud 9, The Seagull, The Provok'd Wife, King Lear, The Misanthrope, Major Barbara, Filumena* and *Kafka's Dick*. Work for the RSC includes: *Family Reunion, Henry V, The Duchess of Malfi, Hamlet, The Lieutenant of Inishmore, Julius Caesar* and *A Midsummer Night's Dream*.

● soho theatre

- ● **Produces new work**
- ● **Discovers and nurtures new writers**
- ● **Targets and develops new audiences**

Soho Theatre creates and enables daring and original new work that challenges the status quo by igniting the imaginations of writers, artists and audiences. We initiate new conversations with London and the wider world through projects that celebrate creative participation, internationalism and freedom of expression. We nurture a socially and culturally broad audience's appetite for theatre and create a buzz around theatre as a living and relevant art form.

'a foundry for new talent . . . one of the country's leading producers of new writing'   Evening Standard

Soho Theatre has a unique Writers' Centre which offers an invaluable resource to emerging theatre writers. The nation's only unsolicited script-reading service, we report for free on over 2,000 plays per year. Through the Verity Bargate Award, the Writers' Attachment Programme, and a host of development programmes and workshops we aim to develop groundbreaking writers and artists to broaden the definition of new theatre writing. Our learning and participation programme Soho Connect includes the innovative Under 11s scheme, the Young Writers' Group (18-25s), Script Slam and an annual site-specific theatre piece with the local community.

Alongside our theatre productions, Soho Theatre presents a high profile late night programme with a mixture of groundbreaking comedy and performance from leading and emergent artists. We also curate talks and other events, encouraging the conversation to spill over into our new and reasonably priced Soho Theatre Bar.

Contemporary, comfortable, air-conditioned and accessible, Soho Theatre is busy from early morning to late at night.

'London's coolest theatre by a mile'   Midweek

● soho theatre

21 Dean Street
London W1D 3NE
Admin: 020 7287 5060
Box Office: 0870 429 6883
www.sohotheatre.com

Soho Theatre Bar

The new Soho Theatre Bar is a comfortable and
affordable place to meet in central London

The Terrace Bar

The Terrace Bar on the second floor serves
a range of soft and alcoholic drinks

Email information list

For regular programme updates and offers visit
www.sohotheatre.com

Hiring the theatre

Soho Theatre has a range of rooms and space for hire.
Please contact the theatre on 020 7287 5060
or go to www.sohotheatre.com for further details.

● soho theatre

The Soho Theatre Development Campaign

Soho Theatre receives core funding from Arts Council England, London. In order to provide as diverse a programme as possible and expand our audience development and outreach work, we rely upon additional support from trusts, foundations, individuals and businesses.

All of our major sponsors share a common commitment to developing new areas of activity and encouraging creative partnerships between business and the arts.

We are immensely grateful for the invaluable support from our sponsors and donors and wish to thank them for their continued commitment.

Soho Theatre has a Friends Scheme in support of its education programme and work developing new writers and reaching new audiences. To find out how to become a Friend of Soho Theatre, contact the development department on 020 7478 0109, email development@sohotheatre.com or visit www.sohotheatre.com.

Sponsors: Angels The Costumiers, Arts & Business, Bloomberg, International Asset Management, Rathbones, TEQUILA\London

Major Supporters and Education Patrons: Tony and Rita Gallagher • Nigel Gee • Paul Hamlyn Foundation • Roger Jospé • Jack and Linda Keenan • John Lyon's Charity • The Pemberton Foundation • The Foundation for Sport and the Arts • Carolyn Ward • The Harold Hyam Wingate Foundation • The Harold Hyam Wingate Foundation

Soho Business Members: Goodman Derrick • Ilovesoho.com

Trusts and Foundations: Anonymous • The Andor Charitable Trust • The Sydney & Elizabeth Corob Charity • The Earmark Trust • Hyde Park Place Estate Charity • The Mackintosh Foundation • The Rose Foundation • Leopold de Rothschild Charitable Trust • The Royal Victoria Hall Foundation • Saddlers' Company • Teale Charitable Trust • Bruce Wake Charitable Trust

Support for Backstage Services: Diana Toeman

Dear Friends: Anonymous • Jill and Michael Barrington • David Day • John Drummond • Daniel Friel • Madeleine Hamel • Steve Hill • Michael and Mimi Naughton • Hannah Pierce • Nicola Stanhope

Good Friends and Friends: Thank you also to the many Soho Friends we are unable to list here. For a full list of our patrons, please visit www.sohotheatre.com

Registered Charity: 267234

Leaves of Glass

Leaves of Grass

'We are the veil
that veils us
from ourselves.'

R. D. Laing

'Commit a crime, and the earth
is made of glass.'

Wallace Stevens

'My secrets cry aloud.'

Theodore Roethke

Characters

Steven
Barry
Debbie
Liz

Steven, *twenty-seven.*

Steven I remember . . . one Sunday morning Dad surprised us. 'Get in the car, boys.' Barry asked, 'Where we going, Dad?' 'A surprise.' I sit in the front seat because I'm the oldest. Fifteen. Barry's in the back getting all excited and jabbering away. He acts a bit young for his age sometimes. He's ten.

Slight pause.

Dad parks the car and says, 'Everybody out!' Seagulls. Barry asks if we're near the seaside. Dad laughs and takes Barry's hand. He goes to take mine but I pull it away. I'm not a kid. We walk down a street. Barry is doing that half-skipping thing and tugging Dad's arm. I tell Barry to calm down. It's one thing to be happy but you don't have to broadcast it to the whole world, do you. Well, *do* you?

Slight pause.

Barry says, 'Look! The Thames!' And there it is. We're right by the river. And then I see – silver! Big silver things across the water. I know what it is. Dad was talking about it last week. The Thames Barrier. Dad explained how if the river gets too high the Barrier would lift up these . . . these – like big doors or something. And it would hold all the water back. Barry said, 'I'd like to see that, Dad.' And, hey presto, here we are. Dad usually gives Barry what he wants. Barry's his favourite. I don't mind. I'm Mum's favourite, so it sort of balances out. Well, don't it? Barry says the Barrier looks like a row of silver pyramids. I tell him not really, because a pyramid has to be pyramid-shaped. And those silver things are shaped like . . . well, not pyramids. Barry says he's gonna do a drawing of it for Dad when he gets home. Dad says he'd love a drawing of silver pyramids. Barry's good at drawing.

Slight pause.

And then . . . then this gust of wind comes along – real strong – and . . . and Dad – he grabs hold of my hand. So sudden.

So tight. His nails dig in. I try to pull away but Dad just holds tighter and tighter. I look at him. The scar by his left eye is sort of twitching. Like it does when Mum's shouting at him and he don't say a single word back. I say, 'Dad . . . you're hurting me!' But still he won't let go. I can see he's holding Barry's hand just as hard. Barry's face is all screwed up. Again I say, 'Dad! You're hurting me.' Again his grip gets tighter. It's as if . . . as if Dad's afraid the gust of wind is going to blow me and Barry away . . . and he'll lose us for ever.

2

Barry's flat.

Barry, twenty-two, is on floor, **Steven** standing.

Barry   Not going there.

Steven   Barry?

Barry   Don't make me . . . don't . . .

Steven's mobile rings.

Answers it.

Hi, Jan . . . At Barry's . . . Yeah, yeah, he's here – Eh? . . . What we expected. Had to knock the door in again. Well, the bloke downstairs did.

Barry   I don't want to!

Steven   Hear him? – Eh? . . . I *have* tried – Barry? . . . Barry?

Barry moans.

Steven   You see? Out to the fucking world – Eh? . . . I'll stay till he surfaces. Cancel everything for the rest of the day – Eh? . . . He's my brother, Jan, what else can I do?

Barry   He'll hurt me!

Steven   Barry? . . . Jesus! He reeks of vomit . . . Oh, it's not just drink, Jan. Don't know. *Don't want to know* – Oh, and Jan.

Not a word in the office. If anyone asks any questions, tell them . . . tell them . . . Yeah. Thanks.

Barry *wakes with a cry.*

Barry No! No!

Steven It's all right, brov.

Barry Steve!

Steven At least he knows me.

Barry Who're you talking to? Mr Ghost?

Steven Here we go – There is no Mr Ghost, brov.

Barry What you talking to that fucking bastard for?

*Grabs **Steven**'s mobile.*

Barry I'm dead, Mr Ghost. Leave me alone.

Steven Stop it, Barry.

Grabs mobile back.

Janis, I'll phone you back.

Hangs up.

Pull yourself together, brov.

Barry If we . . . we stick together we can beat Mr Ghost.

Steven I'll make you some coffee.

Barry We can . . . we can get weapons. Broken bottles. Sticks with . . . with nails sticking out like . . . like medieval things. We can beat him. Together.

Steven Jesus, Barry, where is everything? No coffee. Tea.

Barry We can make Mr Ghost bleed. We can open his head and – Fuck! His brains will spill out. His mind. Cockroaches. Worms. Maggots. Don't look at it, brov. You don't like things like that.

Steven Brov, it's all right. Calm down.

Barry   Steve! Brov! We can chop Mr Ghost into tiny pieces and . . . and – mincemeat. We can scoop Mr Ghost up and – My bucket and spade. We can scoop Mr Ghost up with the spade and put him in the – Mr Ghost'll fill the bucket. Don't look, brov. It'll make you feel sick. I'll cover it with this.

Takes off T-shirt.

Is that better, brov?

Steven   Yes, yes. Thank you.

Barry   We can take the bucketful of Mr Ghost to . . . where? The garden, brov. We'll bury it behind Dad's shed. We'll have to make sure Mum don't see us, won't we, brov. You keep watch, brov. I'll dig the hole. I'll put Mr Ghost in the hole – Don't look, brov! I'll cover him up and then . . . then – Oh, brov. Brov?

Steven   What, Barry?

Barry   What if Mr Ghost grows?

Steven   Grows?

Barry   Like a tree.

Steven   He won't.

Barry   He might. We'll go out one morning and we'll see a finger poking out of the earth. Then more fingers. Like leaves. Then a hand. A wrist. An arm. Bigger and bigger. Mr Ghost'll grow like a . . . a tree. We can't let that happen, brov. We've got to chop the tree down. Cut the tree up.

Steven   All right, all right. It's chopped. Cut.

Barry   But – oh, brov! Brov!

Steven   What?

Barry   The chopped-up bits of Mr Ghost's tree. What'll we do with all the chopped-up bits?

Steven   We won't look at them.

Barry They'll still be there, brov. They'll still – Bury them! Shall we bury them, brov?

Steven Okay, okay.

Barry If we bury all the bits, then – oh, brov. They might all grow into even more Mr Ghost trees – oh, look, brov. Look.

Steven What?

Barry We're in a forest of Mr Ghost trees. We're never gonna get out.

3

Steven*'s house.*

Steven *is looking out of window.*

Debbie*, thirty-three, enters with shopping.*

Debbie Oh! You scared me.

Steven Sorry.

Debbie Thought you was at the office.

Steven I was.

Debbie I've walked miles.

Steven I've been ringing you.

Debbie Oh?

Checks mobile.

Dead. Sorry – Anything wrong?

Steven Wrong?

Debbie You don't usually ring.

Steven I just wanted to . . . to . . .

Debbie Oh, my feet.

Kicks shoes off.

Steven   I rang Barry.

Debbie   Oh?

Steven   Sounded like he was out somewhere.

Debbie   Perhaps he's enjoying himself, Steven. That's what most people do on a Saturday. They let their hair down. They don't lock themselves in a bloody office all day.

Steven   I'm not in an office. I'm here.

Debbie   Why're you here? What're doing?

Steven   I'm . . . I'm looking out the window.

Debbie   At what? Cement mixers. Scaffolding.

Steven   It's not that bad.

Debbie   Worse.

Steven   Not if you're careful where you look.

Debbie   My head! Jesus!

Steven   You can imagine everything's finished.

Debbie   Steven.

Steven   That shadow.

Debbie   Steve.

Steven   It's perfect.

Debbie   I'm pregnant.

Slight pause.

Steven   When?

Debbie   Now. I'm pregnant now.

Steven   But . . .

Debbie   Ain't it good news? The best. I couldn't wait to tell you. We can start decorating that spare room. Like we said.

Steven   What did we say?

Debbie   Nursery.

Steven   We said that?

Debbie   I've seen the perfect cot. Covered in stars.

Steven   Debbie? You're sure?

Debbie   Sure?

Steven   Baby.

Debbie   Yes. Yes. Confirmed this afternoon.

Steven   Confirmed?

Debbie   At the hospital.

Steven   I thought . . . I thought . . .

Debbie   You thought? You thought?

Steven   Your sister? Shopping?

Debbie   I was. We were.

Indicates shopping.

Steven   So you . . .

Debbie   Shopped. Then hospital.

Steven   With Chloe?

Debbie   With Chloe – New handbag!

Steven   But . . .

Debbie   But?

Slight pause.

Oh, I need a bloody bath.

Steven   Did Chloe go with you?

Debbie   You said it's what you wanted, Steven.

Steven   . . . What?

Debbie   A baby.

Steven   Well, it's . . . did I say . . . ?

Debbie   Tick-tock.

Steven   What?

Debbie   Body clock.

Steven   Oh. Yes.

Slight pause.

Debbie   Chloe *said* you'd be like this.

Steven   Like what?

Debbie   This! . . . We were walking out of the hospital and I said, 'Ooh, I can't wait to tell Steve,' and she sort of went, 'Mmm,' in that way she does, and I said, 'What's that supposed to mean?' and she said, 'He'll just give you that look of his, Debs,' and I said, 'He won't, Chloe,' and she said, 'He will, Debbie,' and now I've told you and . . . You are! Look!

Steven   What?

Debbie   That! . . . What's it called again?

Steven   It's got a *name*?

Debbie   Something to do with war.

Steven   War? You've been talking to Barry.

Debbie   No. Chloe.

Steven   What's Chloe know about war?

Debbie   When . . . when she was in that play. Remember?

Steven   No.

Debbie   The raped girl thing.

Steven   What raped girl thing?

Debbie   Soldiers burst into that girl's house. Raped her. Shot her. And the girl's parents. Then set fire to the whole caboodle and went back to base camp calm as cucumbers.

Steven   That.

Debbie   What people are capable of, eh? Awful. Makes you think . . . Bath!

Steven   The 'look', Debbie?

Debbie   What?

Steven   This look I'm supposed to have.

Debbie   Vietnam. Iraq. Some place. – 'Thousand-yard stare'! That's it. That's you.

Steven   Me?

Debbie   You're still doing it! What bloody battle you been in, Steve?

Steven   What?

Debbie   Any massacres at the office lately? Eh? Gang rapes in the storeroom?

Steven   I don't know why you –

Debbie   I rush home from the fucking hospital. Best news ever. Other men'd – they'd jump for joy and . . . whatever. You? Oh no! Jesus. I didn't expect a . . . a . . . Not from you. Never from you. But a kiss. A simple little kiss. Is that too much to . . . ? Jesus.

Slight pause.

Steven *kisses* **Debbie**.

4

Liz's *house.*

Steven *and* **Debbie** *are seated.*

Liz, *fifty-three, enters with tray.*

Liz   My grandmother used to tell me –

Steven   Careful, Mum.

Liz   I can manage – He thinks I'm a whatsit.

Debbie   Damsel in distress.

Steven   I don't.

Liz   I've buried two parents and a husband, I think I'm capable of carrying some tea and biscuits.

Debbie   Hear, hear!

Steven   Debbie don't take sugar any more, Mum.

Liz   I know, I know.

Debbie   I can speak for myself.

Liz   One without the spoon, luv.

Debbie *takes cup and saucer.*

Liz   Biscuits?

Debbie   No thanks, Liz.

Liz   What was I saying?

Steven   Grandmother.

Liz   Teeth!

Steven   Teeth?

Liz   Women used to have one out. Every time.

Steven   Every time what?

Liz   They got pregnant.

Steven   No.

Liz   He thinks I'm stupid.

Steven   I don't.

Debbie   I've heard about this. My sister told me.

Liz   You see?

Offers tray to **Steven**.

Liz   Take it then, take it.

Steven   What one?

Liz   Any, any.

Steven *takes a cup of tea.*

Liz   Biscuit.

Steven   I'm fine.

Liz   I've brought them in now.

Steven *takes a biscuit.*

Debbie   Calcium.

Liz   Bingo!

Steven   What?

Debbie   Woman's teeth used it all up.

Liz   Calcium.

Debbie   Baby's bones wouldn't grow.

Steven   Old wives' tale.

Debbie   They still bloody *did* it, for fuck's sake.

Pause.

Liz   Oh! I've seen the perfect little cot for the baby.

Steven   Really?

Liz   Cherubs all over. Gorgeous.

Steven   Sounds great.

Debbie   We've already got a cot, Liz.

Steven   It ain't been delivered yet.

Debbie   It will be.

Steven   We can cancel.

Debbie   You bloody chose it.

Pause.

Liz   Oh! Your brother told me how thrilled he was about being an uncle. Thrilled! He can't wait. He says he's gonna do a painting soon as it's born.

Debbie *sips tea and winces.*

Debbie   Ugh! Liz.

Liz   Sugar?

Debbie *nods.*

Liz   Sorry, luv – Try yours, Steve.

Steven *sips tea.*

Steven   Sugar.

Liz   Typical.

Debbie *puts cup and saucer back on tray, takes another.*

Liz   Gran saw this woman held down once. Her husband grabbed some pliers and yanked three teeth out in one go. The screams. Blood.

Steven   Mum!

Liz   What?

Indicates **Debbie**.

Debbie   Jesus – I'm pregnant, not ill.

Liz   He thinks you're a shrinking violet.

Debbie   It's *him* who's the shrinking violet.

Liz   He is.

Steven   I'm not.

Debbie   You're squeamish.

Steven   Squeamish?

Liz   You are.

Debbie   He can't look at any of the books I've bought.

Steven   I do.

Debbie   Not the pictures.

Liz   His dad was the same. Passed out in the delivery room. Cracked his forehead. Needed stitches and everything. Frank was too sensitive. Bless him.

Dog barks.

Oh, not again.

Steven   I'll go and complain if you like.

Liz   It gets worse when you complain.

Steven   I'll write to the landlords.

Liz   It's the bloody landlords who're behind it.

Steven   No.

Liz   They want me out.

Steven   Mum.

Liz   They're losing money, rent I pay.

Steven   You're a good tenant.

Liz   What's *that* matter?

Debbie   Turn this place into flats – they'd make a fortune.

Liz   Greed.

Debbie   That's what it is.

Liz   Greed.

Debbie *sips tea.*

Debbie   Ugh! Liz.

Liz   Oh no. Not all of . . . ? What have I . . . ? The dog! They're gonna make my life . . . unbearable . . . All night

sometimes. No rest. Have I been a bad person? Why is this . . . ?
Have I been a bad mother?

Steven   Here, let me help –

Liz   I'm all right.

Steven   But you're gonna drop the –

Liz   Don't!

They all freeze.

The tray rattles.

Dog continues to bark.

5

Steven's *office.*

Steven *and* **Barry**.

Barry   I owe you an explanation.

Steven   Forget it, Barry.

Barry   I can't. We're brothers. You trusted me and I let you
down.

Steven   No.

Barry   Please, Steve. I can't rest until I . . . Please.

Slight pause.

It was really shitty weather this morning. Early. You see it?

Steven   Yeah.

Barry   Grey sky. Grey pavement. Grey people. It was like some
wicked witch had come along and – Shazam! All colour sucked
out. You know those old photos from the First World War?

Steven   What?

Barry   The trenches.

Steven   Those.

Barry   That's what it felt like. This morning. Shot-at-dawn weather. Waiting-to-be-executed weather. That's what they should call a morning like that. On the weather forecast or whatever. 'It's gonna be in-the-trenches weather this morning.' Then we'd all know what they mean. Well, I would. Would you, brov?

Steven   Well, I will now.

Barry   They shot boys. Shell-shocked boys. You know that?

Steven   Terrible.

Barry   The boys were crying, but the men still – Ready! Aim! . . . What was I saying?

Steven   . . . Miserable morning.

Barry   Bloody miserable. And I was standing on that corner where I always stand. Waiting for Jacko and Marky boy. And they were a bit late and –

Steven   That's it!

Barry   What?

Steven   Why didn't you tell me they were late?

Barry   Oh, no. No. It was nothing, brov.

Steven   I'd've been in a bad mood too.

Barry   Few minutes.

Steven   Punctuality.

Barry   Steve. Please. Jacko and Marky boy being late – a few minutes. That's all. It ain't got nothing to do with . . . what happened later. Okay?

Slight pause.

I see the truck coming down the road and Jacko gives his usual three beeps and I squeeze in next to Marky boy and . . . and . . . we drive off and . . . and . . .

Slight pause.

Steven   What, brov?

Barry   You'll think I'd been drinking.

Steven   I won't.

Barry   Cos I've packed it in. All of it.

Steven   I know.

Barry   You know that, don't you?

Steven   Yes . . . I know.

Barry   No drink. Nothing.

Steven   I'm proud of you. We're *all* proud.

Barry   You are?

Steven   Of course.

Barry   Debbie too.

Steven   Of course Debbie too.

Slight pause.

Barry   Guess what they looked like?

Steven   Who?

Barry   Jacko and Marky boy.

Steven   I . . . I'm not sure what you –

Barry   You know those photos from Auschwitz?

Steven   Auschwitz?

Barry   Those skull-like faces. All teeth and eye sockets.

Steven   Those.

Barry   On their way to the fucking gas chamber.

Phone rings.

Steven   Yes? . . . Would you like some tea, brov?

Barry   No, no, I'm fine.

Steven   He's fine. We're *both* fine . . . Eh? . . . Postpone it . . . An hour . . . I'll phone him . . . Email it through . . . Three weeks at the most . . . Well, if there's a complaint they can put it in writing . . . Thanks, Janis.

Barry   She's a good one – Janis.

Steven   Yes.

Barry   Best secretary you've ever had, I reckon. Next to . . . what was her name? Paulette?

Steven   Yes. Paulette was good.

Barry   Better than Kelly.

Steven   Yes.

Barry   Debbie was bloody good, though.

Steven   Yes. Debbie was very good.

Barry   No, she wasn't.

Steven   No.

Barry   Not as bad as me, though. I can crash a computer by just looking at it. I've been born in the wrong time, I reckon. Wrong era. Few hundred years ago – that would have suited me. Sort of Renaissance times. That's more like five hundred, ain't it?

Steven   I'm . . . not sure . . .

Barry   Wine out of goblets and candlelight and – Dad liked candlelight, didn't he, brov? Remember the candles in the shed?

Steven   Yes.

Barry   That's where I get it from, I reckon. The romantic streak. I should've been mates with Byron and Shelley and all that lot. White frilly shirts and screwing buxom wenches in taverns.

Steven   And catching syphilis.

Barry   I've had that anyway.

Steven   No cure. Your nose drops off.

Barry   Who needs a nose? It's an affectation. Take it.

They laugh.

I like it when you laugh. Come here, brov.

Hugs **Steven**.

Barry   Fuck, you're all tense. I'll give you a head massage. Come on.

Steven   Not now, brov.

Barry   Later?

Steven   Yes. Later.

Barry   You won't let me forget now.

Steven   No, no.

Slight pause.

Barry   She showed me the picture.

Steven   What? Who?

Barry   Debbie. The picture of the scan.

Steven   Oh.

Barry   The baby.

Steven   Yes, yes.

Barry   Beautiful. Baby's little legs. Its heart.

Steven   Barry . . . why did you run away from the job this morning?

Barry   Oh. Right.

Slight pause.

We drove to the estate. Me and Jacko and Marky boy. They're still concentration camp victims. I can't understand a fucking word they're prattling on about. Jewish. They must be speaking that. Do you speak Jewish or Yiddish?

Steven   I don't know.

Barry   I think it's Yiddish. 'My Yiddisher Mamma.' Ain't that a song?

Steven   Barry. Please.

Slight pause.

Barry   I get the water blaster from the back of the truck. I see Jacko pointing at the wall we're gonna clean. Pointing with this thin, twig-like finger. Know what it reminds me of, brov? Hansel and Gretel. When the kids are getting fattened up. To be cooked by the witch. This witch puts the kids in a cage and gives the children lots of chocolate. Goes on for months and months. Then the witch asks one of the kids – Hansel, I think. Or was it Gretel? Dunno. She asks one of them to put their finger through the cage so the witch can make sure the kid is fat enough for eating. And the kid sticks a twig through. And the witch thinks the kid's all thin. Or something like that. I dunno. Sometimes you think you remember a story, but you don't. Like when you think of your favourite film. A film you saw when you was a kid, say. For years and years you've been saying, 'I love that bit where . . . ' such-and-such happens. And then you see the film again and – it don't happen like that at all. And other bits of the film – this film you saw a million times when you was a kid – you'd forgotten completely. It's like you're seeing them for the first time. Don't you find that, brov?

Steven   Barry.

Barry   Yes, brov?

Steven   Tell me . . . tell me what happened this morning.

Barry   . . . A shaft of light.

Steven   What?

Barry   It breaks through the grey clouds like a . . . a . . . Fuck knows. But it breaks through and it − Spotlight! It hits the wall. The graffiti. And it . . . oh, brov, I see . . . I fucking see . . .

Steven   What?

Barry   Colour! The wall! It's so bright and − Stained glass! Dazzling. If it was music it would've blown my eardrums out. They'd still be ringing now. Like after a concert. My eyes are ringing. It was like a good witch has come along and − Shazam! Brought colour back! Guess what it was of?

Steven   What?

Barry   The grafitti.

Steven   I don't know.

Barry   An explosion.

Steven   Oh! Yes . . . I remember now.

Barry   Go on.

Steven   Something to do with that bomb that went off.

Barry   Last year.

Steven   In the local market.

Barry   Outside the supermarket.

Steven   Someone with a bomb in a rucksack.

Barry   Boom!

Steven   Terrible.

Barry   A kid was killed.

Steven   Lucky there wasn't more.

Barry   Not lucky for the kid.

Steven   No.

Barry   The suicide bomber.

Steven   Oh. Well . . .

Barry   They found his head in a supermarket trolley, you know.

Steven   No!

Barry   . . . No. I made that up. Good image though.

Steven   Good image?

Barry   Can't remember where they found the head. But I know they *did* find it cos someone went to identify it. Remember?

Steven   No.

Barry   The bomber's dad. They spoke to him on the telly. He looked like . . . well, like he'd just seen the severed head of his son. He was only fifteen.

Steven   Who?

Barry   The bomber.

Steven   Really?

Barry   He came from Leyton. Just down the road. Remember that interview with his mum?

Steven   No.

Barry   She said how her son was the most considerate child a mother could ever have in the whole world.

Steven   Goes to show.

Barry   What?

Steven   That . . . he wasn't.

Barry   Not really. He could still be the most considerate child in the whole world to his mum and a right evil bastard to everyone else in the world, couldn't he?

Steven   I suppose he could.

Barry   He was in the graffiti.

Steven   Who?

Barry The bomber.

Steven Yes, yes, I remember now.

Barry There was all this burning wreckage around him. The flames were all cadmium yellow and vermilion. And there was this crowd standing round watching it. And all the firelight was reflected in their faces. In their eyes. And out of the flames . . . out of the smoke of the flames. The kid. The kid who died. And he had wings. He was an angel. And he was flying up to the sky. And the sky was all deep blue. Marine. And there were hundreds of stars – Dad told us once stars were sort of doors . . . gateways to death. Remember that?

Steven He . . . he didn't tell me.

Barry He did. I was there.

Steven He didn't.

Barry He did.

Steven Okay, okay, he did. But I've forgot.

Barry That's why Van Gogh painted stars. The painter. Ya know?

Steven I know who Van Gogh is, yes.

Barry Stars like . . . like rainbow whirlpools. Everyone looks at the painting and goes, 'Ooh, how pretty. How beautiful.' And it's a sky full of death. Well, I suppose it is beautiful. Some things are, ain't they, brov? Terrible and beautiful at the same time.

Steven Barry. All I want to know is –

Barry I couldn't blast away all that colour, brov.

Steven You . . . couldn't?

Barry It'd be a fucking sin.

Steven A sin?

Barry Why'd they wanna get rid of it anyway? It's a tribute.

Steven   People felt it was . . . glorifying the event.

Barry   Glorifying?

Steven   Turning the dead boy into a sort of martyr.

Barry   Ooh, cult of death.

Steven   Yes.

Barry   Nasty, cult of death. Eh, brov? We don't want that, do we, brov?

Steven   No.

Barry   People killing themselves all over the place. There'd be a mad rush to do it. 'Me first!' 'No! Me first!'

Slight pause.

I ran.

Steven   You . . . ?

Barry   I fucking ran, brov. I couldn't blast away all that colour. I couldn't turn the world all grey again. I yelled back at Jacko and Marky boy, 'I ain't gonna get turned into soap. I'm no fucking lampshade!'

Phone rings.

Steven   Everything's fine . . . Eh? . . . Well, tell him we need three days or he can go somewhere else . . . Does he want it done quick or does he want it done properly?

Hangs up.

Barry   Your mind, brov. It's like a . . . a laser. You know that? It's full of all that . . . energy. If your brain was an animal, you know what it'd be? Eh? A shark. Sharks have to keep swimming otherwise they die. Sharks never sleep. That's what they say, anyway. Might be a loud of bollocks. I'd still like to believe it, though. Wouldn't you, brov? Eh?

Steven   I . . . don't . . .

Barry   A world without shark-dreams.

Slight pause.

Steven   Why don't you take a few days off?

Barry   I want to quit, Steve.

Steven   What? When?

Barry   Now.

Steven   No.

Barry   It's not fair on you.

Steven   Don't worry about me.

Barry   This is *your* business.

Steven   *Our* business.

Barry   What the fuck did I do?

Steven   A lot.

Barry   Nothing. *You* built it up. From scratch. My brother –
The Man with The Plan.

Steven   You're part of that plan.

Barry   I'm a joke.

Steven   No.

Barry   The way people here look at me.

Steven   How do they look?

Barry   Charity case.

Steven   No one thinks that.

Barry   You've always known how to make money, ain't you,
brov?

Steven   I've worked hard, yes.

Barry   I know you feel it.

Steven   Feel what?

Barry   We're . . . drifting.

Steven   Drifting?

Barry   Fuck, Steve. It's about time. That's what I'm saying.
We've got to talk about it.

Steven   About what?

Barry   Jesus.

Steven   Tell me.

Barry   No. *You* did it. *You* tell *me*.

Steven   Did what?

Barry   *You* should be the one.

Steven   Barry.

Barry   What?

Steven   What did I do?

Slight pause.

What is it you think I did?

6

Steven *and* **Debbie***'s house.*

Steven *and* **Debbie** *are having dinner.*

Debbie   My sister saw a UFO.

Steven   Really?

Debbie   She was in some playground somewhere.

Steven   Oh?

Debbie   Her and this new bloke of hers. They climbed over
this fence or whatever and got inside. Night.

Steven   She'll get in trouble one day.

Debbie   I've told her.

Steven   Were they pissed?

Debbie   Swears they weren't. But you know Chloe.

Steven   I know Chloe.

Pause.

Debbie   Is the lamp too bright?

Steven   I . . . I don't know.

Debbie   Think it might be.

Steven   Perhaps a bit.

Turns lamp off.

Better?

Steven   Much.

Debbie   Chloe says they had a twirl on the whatnot then flopped in the sandpit.

Steven   Didn't think playgrounds had sandpits any more.

Debbie   Oh?

Steven   Danger hazard.

Debbie   *Danger* hazard?

Steven   Dog poo.

Debbie   Eating, Steven, eating.

Steven   Sorry.

Slight pause.

When was this?

Debbie   What?

Steven   The UFO.

Debbie   Oh. Last week sometime, I think.

Steven   You went out with her last week.

Debbie   I know I did.

Steven   Twice. Till late.

Debbie   So?

Steven   So . . . Chloe likes lots of late nights.

Debbie   She likes to have fun. She likes to . . . to go wild now and again. She'd end up in a fucking straitjacket otherwise.

Slight pause.

They eat.

Pause.

Is it a bit dark now?

Steven   I . . . whatever you think.

Debbie   Can you see your food?

Steven   Yes.

Debbie   You *can*?

Steven   Can you?

Slight pause.

They eat.

Debbie   Anyway, they were gazing up at the sky. In this danger hazard of a sandpit. In each other's arms. It was all very romantic. Horny. You know? Bloody horny?

Steven   . . . Yes.

Debbie   And then . . . then they see something in the sky. Right above them.

Steven   Jesus.

Debbie   I know. She said there weren't no flashing lights or anything.

Steven   Really?

Debbie   Nothing like the films.

Steven   Really?

Debbie   And she said it was dead quiet. You couldn't hear an engine or anything.

Steven   Jesus.

Debbie   I know. She said the UFO was just this round-shaped . . . blackness.

Steven   Blackness?!

Debbie   What the fuck's wrong with you?

Pause.

Steven   . . . Sorry?

Debbie   Stop being so fucking . . . interested.

Steven   But I *am* interested.

Pause.

Debbie   I can't see my food.

Turns lamp on.

They eat.

Pause.

Steven   When did you show Barry the photo?

Debbie   Eh? What?

Steven   Barry said you showed him the photo of the scan.

Debbie   I . . . yes, I did.

Steven   When?

Debbie   I don't know. Day before yesterday.

Steven   He came round?

Debbie   Yes.

Steven   Out of the blue?

Debbie   No. You asked him to.

Steven   I didn't.

Debbie   You did. I heard you on the phone.

Steven   No.

Debbie   You asked him to clear some space in the cellar. For your mum's stuff. The stuff we're storing when she moves.

Steven   Oh . . .

Debbie   Oh!

They eat.

Pause.

I'm sure we've got rats.

Steven   Where?

Debbie   In the cellar.

Steven   No.

Debbie   Well, I heard something.

Steven   Not rats.

Debbie   I had enough of rats when I was a kid. Afraid to let my foot slip from under the covers in case my toes were nibbled off.

They eat.

Pause.

This light's giving me a fucking headache.

Turns lamp off.

That better. For you? What d'you think? This – ?

Turns lamp on.

Or this?

Turns lamp off.

This?

Lamp on.

Or this?

Off.

This?

On.

Or this?

Off.

This?

On.

Or this?

Off.

7

Steven   I remember . . . I'm fifteen years old. I'm in the back
garden. Cold. Stars. I'm looking through the window of Dad's
shed. My breath mists the glass. I hear distant bangs. See
sparkles in the sky. It's firework night. We're going to make our
own little bonfire in the garden. Dad – he's got a big tin drum
and he's put all sorts of stuff in it. He's gonna light it. Mum's
making potatoes in their jackets. I wipe the mist off the
window. Dad's at the table in his shed. Dad's got this silver . . .
candleholder – candelabrum! The candles are all flickering.
Dad says candlelight helps him think. Dad's very still. Dad's
looking at his notebooks. Dad's got lots of little notebooks.
They're full of his scribbles and doodles. He's been keeping
them for years and years. Since he was a kid. He's got about
twenty of them. Some of them are so old they're Sellotaped

together. No one's allowed to look at the notebooks. Dad keeps them in a tin box. An old biscuit tin. There's a painting on the top. Snow. A frozen lake. People in old-fashioned clothes skating. I'm about to tap on the window when I see Dad's face. It looks odd somehow. All puffy and red. Like he's freezing. It can't be that cold in there. He's got a little gas heater. I can see the blue flame. I keep quiet. Don't know why. Dad picks up the notebooks. All of them. He walks out of the shed. He don't see me. He goes over to the tin drum and he drops the notebooks into it. Then he piles bits of wood on top. Then he strikes a match. Then he holds the match above the tin drum. He looks so calm now. All the red and puffiness has gone. He drops the match into the tin drum. I want to cry out, 'Dad! What're you doing? That's all your scribblings and doodles you're burning up!' But I don't. I just watch as – whoosh! Flames. Barry rushes out of the house with the fireworks. Mum rushes out with the jacket potatoes. I look at Dad. There's lots of sparks all round his head. I remember thinking . . . they look like stars.

8

Liz's *house.*

Steven *and* **Barry**.

Barry *drops box.*

Steven   Jesus.

Barry   Sorry.

Steven   You've got to be careful, Barry.

Barry   It slipped.

Steven   Why don't you sit down for a while?

Barry   I want to help.

Steven   You could make us all a cup of tea.

Barry   *You* make a cup of bloody tea. We're ain't in the office now.

Liz *walks in, holding box.*

Liz   What was that noise?

Steven   Nothing.

Barry   I dropped this.

Liz   Oh no.

Goes to box.

What with half my stuff in your brother's cellar and you breaking everything you touch I ain't gonna have much to take with me, am I?

Steven   You'll have plenty, Mum.

Liz   It'll look like plenty cos I'm squeezing a two-bedroom house into a poky flat.

Steven   It's not poky, Mum.

Slight pause.

Did you tell Mum about our old room, brov?

Barry   Eh?

Steven   The wall.

Barry   No.

Liz   What?

Steven   He peeled off some of the wallpaper.

Liz   Really?

Steven   Guess what was underneath.

Slight pause.

Mum?

Liz   What? What?

Steven   Something he'd written.

Barry   When I was a kid.

Steven   He must've been only . . . what? Nine or something?

Barry   Younger. It was when Dad put up that cowboy wallpaper.

Steven   Guess what it was, Mum.

Liz   What – ? Oh, how can I?

Steven (*with* **Barry**)   'Steven and Barry – brothers for ever!'

Barry (*with* **Steven**)   'Steven and Barry – brothers for ever!'

Steven *and* **Barry** *laugh.*

Barry   Mum? Don't you think he's got a great smile. Eh?

Takes smashed framed photo from box.

Liz   Oh no! No! Look!

Steven   Careful, you'll cut yourself.

Liz   I know.

Barry   It's only the glass that's broke.

Steven   The photo's okay.

Barry   You can get it reframed.

Steven   I'll get it done for you.

Liz   This was the last picture your dad took of you both. Remember?

Steven   No.

Barry   I do. We're in the garden.

Steven   Well, I can tell that much.

Barry   It's my tenth birthday. That T-shirt. I drew those stars on it. Remember? With those special pens Dad bought me.

Liz   We *both* bought them for you.

Barry   Each star's a different colour. See? Took me ages. Dad loved it. Said I should start a T-shirt stall and sell 'em. Remember, brov?

Steven   . . . No.

Barry   I wore it all the time after he . . . after he died.

Liz   You used to be such a beautiful boy, Barry.

Slight pause.

Steven   . . . Brov, why don't you take the box downstairs?

Barry   Where shall I . . . ?

Steven   My car.

Throws car keys to **Barry**.

Barry *goes.*

Steven   He's trying his best, Mum.

Liz   If you say so.

Steven   He's not drunk anything for three months.

Liz   He'll start again.

Steven   No. He means it this time.

Liz   He's meant it all the other times. Every other time since he was thirteen.

Steven   He didn't have a drink problem when he was thirteen.

Liz   I imagined the piles of vomit I had to clear up, did I?

Steven   He was a teenager.

Liz   Never had all that trouble with you.

Steven   Barry wasn't trouble.

Liz   He nearly demolished the house that time.

Steven   He didn't!

Liz   He smashed everything, Steven. My glass ornaments. All the things you bought me. Beautiful things. Why must you protect him all the time? It doesn't help, you know.

Steven   Okay, okay.

Liz   It makes him worse.

Slight pause.

Barry would be such a disappointment to your dad.

Steven   Don't, Mum.

Liz   Your dad adored Barry. You know that.

Steven   I know.

Liz   He worshipped the ground that boy walked on.

Slight pause.

Steven   He's hoping to have another exhibition.

Liz   *Another?* When was the first?

Steven   That thing down Bethnal Green Road.

Liz   Doodles Blu-tacked to a wall?

Steven   They weren't Blu-tacked.

Liz   Well, it wasn't an exhibition.

Steven   It was a student show, Mum.

Liz   Student! Ha!

Steven   He got into St Martin's.

Liz   And lasted all of two terms.

Steven   But he *did* get in.

Liz   It's not the *getting* in that matters in life, Steven. It's the *staying* in.

Slight pause.

Ted took me to see an exhibition once.

Steven   Ted?

Liz   From the fruit and veg stall.

Steven   Oh. Him.

Liz   Don't say it like that.

Steven   Like what?

Liz   He treated me lovely. He paid for a taxi all the way there.

Steven   Where?

Liz   This . . . art gallery. Some big building down Piccadilly. You know where I mean.

Steven   I don't.

Liz   You do! Water lilies. That's what the paintings were of. Dreamy. Like looking into that aquarium at the dentist's. *That* was what I call an exhibition. Not Blu-tacked pornography.

Steven   It wasn't pornography.

Liz   What else would you call it?

Steven   There's a . . . a different attitude now, Mum.

Liz   Oh, don't give me all that crap. I was married for fifteen years. I know what sex is.

Steven   Mum.

Liz   Well, I do. And your brother's drawings were not about sex. All those screaming faces. The tears. That's not the sex as I know it. Not me or any normal . . . any decent −

Steven   Don't get yourself worked up.

Liz   You think it's easy for a mum? Eh? Seeing her son do stuff like that? Knowing it came from his head?

Steven   No.

Liz   Well.

Slight pause.

It's like . . . like I've had three sons, not two. There's you. And then there's the two Barrys. There's the Barry *before* your dad died. And then there's the Barry *after* his dad died. You remember the first Barry, Steven? So happy. So clever. Always interested. Asking questions and . . . laughing. He used to laugh all the time. Remember?

Steven   I wish you wouldn't keep going over . . . all this.

Liz   The headmaster told me Barry was the brightest boy in his class. He was always creating something. He could take a sheet of paper and turn it into . . . pure magic. Couldn't he? Eh?

Steven   Yes.

Liz   He made me Christmas and birthday cards by hand. Feathers and flowers stuck to them.

Steven   Grief . . . it affects people in different ways.

Liz   It was the making of you.

Steven   Don't say that.

Liz   It was. You blossomed.

Slight pause.

You notice?

Steven   What?

Liz   Not one bark. Ever since I told the landlords I was moving out – Perfectly silent.

9

Steven   I'm in my bedroom. Barry's making a noise. He's in the bedroom with me. He's kneeling on his bed. He's in his side of the bedroom but he's still bugging me. The carpet's got a sort of ziggy-zaggy pattern, you see, and I've told him that this red line here . . . that's the dividing line between my side

and his side. All his things have to stay on his side of this red
ziggy-zaggy line. Barry – he's pinned a large sheet of paper on
the wall. He's using coloured pencils to draw something. A leaf.
Bright red. From the tree in the garden. Dad gave it to him
and said, 'Look at this! A perfect leaf!' And Barry got all
excited and giggly the way he does. And now he's drawing it –
Huge! Every little vein and . . . and insect bite. Barry's making
those little gaspy noises. He's facing the wall. He's got his back
to me. His hair is all sort of . . . glowing in the sunlight. The
nape of his neck looks pure gold. I can see the shape of his
spine through his T-shirt. He's wearing jeans. There's felt-tip
scribbles on them. His feet are bare. Soles dirty. Barry picks up
a pencil . . . Orange. He shades the leaf some more. Little
gasps. I can't see his face but I know he'll be licking his fucking
lips. Lick, lick. I look at the pencils. Some are very sharp. I want
to stab him in the neck with one. In that pure-gold spot. I want
to really hurt him. Barry looks at me and says, 'Nearly finished.
Dad's gonna love it. What d'ya think, brov?' I look at the giant
red leaf. Then I stand up. Barry's waiting for an answer. I
wonder what he'd do if I stuck a pencil in each fucking eye.
I could do. So easy. Pop. Pop. I walk out of the room without
saying anything. I close the door behind me. I hear Barry
continue to gasp as he draws. It don't bother him if I answer
or not. Nothing bothers him. How can he be so fucking
content all the fucking time? I look down the stairs and –
there's Dad. He's standing by the front door. His hand is on
it like he's about to go out. But he's not going out. He's just
standing there. Very still. I go to say something. But I don't.
Don't know why. I hear Barry call, 'Dad!' Dad jumps. As if
he's just been woken up. 'Dad!' Barry's finished the drawing.
He wants Dad to come and see. Dad opens the front door.
Dad steps outside. A gust of air blows up the stairs. So cold.
That's when I notice Dad's wearing his slippers. He can't be
going out. Not in his slippers. I want to call, say something.
But I don't. Don't know why. Dad closes the door behind him.
I hear Dad open the garden gate and close it. Barry comes out
of the bedroom. 'Where's Dad?' I look at Barry. 'He's gone
out,' I tell him. 'He heard you calling. He said he didn't want
to see your stupid pathetic drawing.' Barry's eyes are filling

with tears. I want him to cry so much. I say, 'Dad said it's time
you forgot all about this stupid art stuff. How you gonna earn
money when you leave school? Eh?' Barry starts crying. He
runs back into the room. I listen to him cry and cry and . . .
I'm not angry with Barry any more. I'm not in a bad mood
about anything. I feel very calm.

10

Barry's *flat.*

Steven *and* **Barry**.

Steven *is in neck brace and holding walking stick.*

Barry   First surprise!

Steven   Okay.

Barry   Don't look.

Steven   I won't.

Barry   Eyes closed.

Steven   Yes, yes.

Barry *reveals a painting.*

Barry   Okay . . . Open.

Steven *opens his eyes.*

Barry   Well?

Steven   Wow!

Pause.

It's big.

Barry   Is it?

Steven   Well . . . it's bigger than . . .

Barry   Something smaller?

Steven   . . . Yes.

Barry   I call it 'Lovesong for the Offspring of Enola Gay'.

Steven   . . . Intriguing.

Barry   Know who Enola Gay was?

Steven   Some pop group or something?

Barry   Hiroshima.

Steven   That.

Barry   The pilot of the aircraft – the aircraft that was gonna drop the bomb . . . forget his name. Don't matter . . . this bomb – this fucking fucking bomb – it's the biggest ever fuck-off bomb ever made, right? Everyone in the world knows. They've done the tests, for chrissakes. In that desert and stuff. The sand – it was turned to glass. You know that, brov? The heat was so fucking intense the desert became a sheet of glass. Like a wicked witch had come along and – Shazam! This fucking bomb . . . this fucking bomb – whole islands were destroyed. You've seen that, brov, ain't ya? You must have. Those islands?

Steven   Yes, yes.

Barry   Boom! Boiled fish in the water. Nuclear fallout whatsit like snow. Sunsets like fucking . . . blood. Like the fucking sky had cut its wrists – And hey! I should know, eh?

Steven   Don't joke about it, Barry.

Barry   And pigs. They put pigs on ships near to the islands. Know why? To see what this new fucking bomb would do to them. Turned them into pork scratchings, that's what it did. So . . . they know what this fucking mega fuck-off bomb can do, right? To islands. To pigs. To cities. People. They know. This pilot who's gonna drop the bomb – he knows. This bomb is one evil fucker. And the pilot has to think of a name for the plane. You with me, brov?

Steven   Yes, yes.

Barry So what does he call it? This evil bird with an egg of fuck-off shit. 'Wings of Terror'? 'Evil Witch Fucker with Fuck-Off Bomb'? No. He calls it 'Enola Gay'. And you know who Enola Gay was?

Steven No, brov.

Barry His fucking mother.

Stumbles.

Steven Careful.

Barry I'm not drunk.

Steven I know.

Barry Not a mouthful. Four months.

Steven I'm proud of you, brov.

Barry You're *all* proud of me, eh?

Steven Of course.

Barry Debbie's proud of me.

Steven . . . Yes.

Barry You'd be annoyed if I started again, wouldn't you, brov?

Steven I'd be . . . upset.

Barry Annoyed.

Steven Disappointed.

Barry You'd want to hit me probably, wouldn't you, brov?

Steven No.

Barry You would.

Steven I wouldn't.

Barry Why don't you whack me in the face with your stick? Knock a few teeth out. Come on!

Slight pause.

Next surprise!

Steven   Okay.

Barry   Don't look!

Steven   I won't.

Barry   Eyes closed?

Steven   Yes, yes.

Barry *goes to wardrobe and puts on a crash helmet.*

Barry   Open.

Steven   Wow!

Barry   Why am I wearing this, do you think?

Steven   . . . You haven't?

Barry   Take a look.

Indicates window.

Steven *goes to window.*

Barry   Surprise!

Steven   Expensive.

Barry   Very.

Steven   How?

Barry   Put the two surprises together.

Steven   You . . . you sold it?

Barry   And . . . and . . .

Opens a sketchbook.

These drawings. Here. Some dealer in Birmingham wants the lot. They're a sequence. You see? Individually they don't make much sense. Composition's all fucked up.

Steven   I wouldn't know.

Barry   Trust me. Fucked up. But when you put them next to each other and . . . it'll start to balance out. Make sense. The same images occur in all of them. Hidden somewhere. You see? A tree here . . . Roots . . . A leaf.

Steven *winces and rubs his knee.*

Barry   Fuck! I should've offered you a seat. Sorry.

Steven   Just a twinge.

Barry   My brother the hero – Here.

Steven *sits.*

Barry   I feel terrible now. You come all the way round here. I ramble on and on – Why didn't you tell me to shut the fuck up, brov?

Steven   I like to hear you talk.

Barry   Ain't even asked how you're feeling.

Steven   Don't worry about it.

Barry   I am worried. Bro! Brov!

Steven   What?

Barry   How you feeling?

Steven   A lot better, thank you.

Barry   Any pain in the neck?

Steven   No, no. All cleared up.

Barry   Why you still wearing that then?

Steven   Just in case.

Barry   In case what?

Steven   In case . . .

Slight pause.

Barry   The bruising?

Steven   All gone.

Barry   So it's just . . . what? The knee?

Steven   Only when I've been standing for too long.

Barry   I'm a thoughtless bastard, ain't I?

Steven   No, no.

Barry   I am, I am. I was just eager to show you –

Steven   I know, I know. And I was eager to see!

Barry   Brov! Shall I get one of my healing crystals?

Steven   Oh . . . I . . .

Barry   It'll help.

Steven   No, it's fine.

Barry   It'll help.

Steven   Go on then.

Barry *gets crystal. He places it on* **Steven***'s knee.*

Barry   How's that feel?

Steven   Mmm.

Barry   Can you feel the energy?

Steven   I'm not sure . . .

Barry   Does it feel warm? Bet it does.

Steven   . . . It does a bit.

Barry   That's the healing energy.

Steven   Really?

Barry   Really. A trauma like you've had – sometimes it can unlock our channels.

Steven   Unlock our channels?

Barry   Just let it happen, brov. Don't resist.

Pause.

Debbie said all your memory has come back, then.

Steven   What – ? Oh. Yes.

Barry   So you remember the crash and everything now.

Steven   Yes, yes.

Barry   You swerved to avoid a kid or something.

Steven   A boy, yes.

Barry   Fuck.

Steven   And he . . . he didn't run out.

Barry   Oh?

Steven   No. He was just sort of . . . there.

Barry   There?

Steven   In the middle of the road – Has Debbie told you all this?

Barry   No, no.

Steven   I turned a corner and – There he is!

Barry   Fuck me!

Steven   Right in front of me. Just staring.

Barry   You've been seeing too many horror films, brov.

Steven   It's not a joke.

Barry   . . . I know. Sorry.

Slight pause.

Crashing into a wall is serious.

Steven   Corrugated iron.

Barry   What?

Steven   It wasn't a wall. It was corrugated iron.

Barry   It could've been a wall.

Steven   It could've. But it wasn't.

Barry   But if it was a wall . . . ooh, shudder, shudder. Eh, brov? You might've beaten me to it. Driving straight into a wall – Splat! Better than the wrists. We'll have to work harder at it, though, brov. Can't keep bodging it, can we? Eh?

Pause.

Steven   When did you speak to her?

Barry   Who?

Steven   Debbie. She told you my memory was back, you said.

Barry   . . . Debbie said you get pissed off when I talk to her.

Steven   I'm not pissed off.

Barry   Are.

Steven   Just curious.

Barry   Oh. Curious – Fuck, I can feel the crystal getting really hot.

Slight pause.

Steven   So . . . when did you . . . ?

Barry   Mmm?

Steven   See Debbie.

Barry   When I went round.

Steven   To the house.

Barry   Yeah.

Slight pause.

Steven   When?

Barry   Eh?

Steven   When did you go round?

Barry   To your place?

Steven   Yes.

Barry   Ooh . . . I forget – Bloody hell, can you feel it, brov? Energy!

Steven   Why did you go round, Barry?

Barry   Round where?

Steven   To the bloody house.

Barry   Brov, if you get wound up it'll divert the healing flow.

Steven   I'm not getting bloody wound up. I just want to know why you went round the bloody house.

Barry   Mum couldn't find something. She wondered if it was in your cellar. I popped round to have a look.

Steven   What couldn't she find?

Barry   I forget now.

Steven   Why didn't Mum ask me to look for whatever it was?

Barry   Said she did.

Steven   Hasn't.

Barry   Lots of times, she said.

Steven   No.

Barry   Perhaps it was one of the things you forgot.

Steven   I forgot bits of the past. Not now.

Barry   There's only one explanation then.

Steven   What?

Barry   Mum's a lying, two-faced manipulative cow.

Slight pause.

Steven   Mum could've phoned Debbie.

Barry   Debbie won't go down the cellar. Not with the rats.

Steven   We ain't got rats – okay, okay, enough.

Stands.

Barry   It feels better, don't it?

Steven   What I don't understand is why . . . why she never tells me when she sees you. Why it always slips out accidentally.

Barry   'Slips out accidentally'?

Steven   Are you fucking her, Barry?

Slight pause.

Well?

Barry *laughs.*

Steven   Don't laugh. Something . . . something's going on. Why'd it take her so long to tell me? About the pregnancy. Eh? She suspected she was pregnant. Not a word. Why wait? What was she waiting for? Debating whether to have it or not? Cos it's not mine. Cos it's yours!

Barry *laughs louder.*

Steven   Shut up! Shut up!

Tears sketchbook.

Barry   Hey! No! Steve!

Tries to stop him.

Brov! For fuck's sake.

Steven *calms.*

Pause.

Steven   I'm . . . I'm sorry.

Barry   Fuck off.

Steven   Are they okay?

Barry   Do they look okay?

Steven   I'll pay you for them.

Barry   That's your fucking answer to everything, ain't it.

Steven   What?

Barry   Money.

Steven*'s mobile rings.*

Steven   Hello . . . What? . . . No, no, tell them . . . it's an estimate only . . . What? . . . I don't know, Jan, I . . . I can't think now. I'll sort it out later . . . Later, Jan! I can't think. Okay? I can't . . . I can't . . .

Hangs up.

Pause.

Barry   It'll be fine, brov. I can do them again.

Steven   You sure?

Barry   Happens all the time.

Slight pause.

Steven   I don't know why I said . . .

Barry   I know.

Steven   You . . . you won't tell Debbie?

Barry   Course not.

Steven   I don't want her to think −

Barry   You can trust me. You know that. Lips sealed.

II

Steven's *house. Night.*

Steven *holds walking stick. No neck brace.*

Debbie *enters.*

Debbie   Steve?

Slight pause.

What the fuck's going on?

Turns television off.

It's the middle of the bloody night – Oh, no! Look!

Sees red stain on white rug.

What's got into you lately? Everything you bloody touch . . .
Broke. Smashed. That clock my sister got us. Still don't know
how I'm gonna tell her. All those little shiny things inside. All
spinning and whirling. Not any more.

Sees **Steven** *pouring drink.*

Debbie   Jesus, you drinking?

Slight pause.

What you drinking for?

Steven   Why'd we buy the fucking stuff if we weren't gonna
drink it?

Debbie   We bought it cos it goes with the cocktail cabinet.

Steven   Why'd we buy the fucking cabinet then?

Debbie   We liked the way it lights up.

Steven   *You* liked the way it lights up!

Debbie   So did you.

Steven   No. I *never* liked it. Do you know, I don't think I like
one fucking thing in this whole fucking house. I don't like the

leather sofa and the glass coffee table and the glass shelves –
Why's there so much fucking glass anyway? It's like living in
a . . . a . . . I dunno. Greenhouse! Ice palace.

Pause.

Debbie   Cranberry juice. This'll stain, you know.

Steven   Another polar bear skinned in vain.

Debbie   It's not polar bear.

Steven   Tell you what, I'll drive you to London Zoo one
night. You can scale the fence and club a bear over the head.
Use one of your five hundred handbags. That gold crocodile-
skin monstrosity that cost a fortune. You can fill it with all the
jewellery you've been buying over the past two years and –
Whack! One dead polar bear.

Debbie   You finished?

Steven   Or . . . or . . . you can kill it by feeding it one of
your chicken-nugget risottos. Or make it listen to you droning
on about your hard-luck fucking childhood and the way you
always dreamed of . . . what was it again? A house with a
swimming pool and barbecues every Sunday and sitting
around in the kitchen with girlfriends nibbling cheesecake and
sipping Chardonnay.

Debbie   Every girl dreams of that.

Steven   No they fucking don't.

Debbie   What? Eh? What, Steve? What? What have I
bloody done? Why are you – ? The past few months you've
been . . . My sister said I should say something. Sit you down
and have a heart to – heart! You! That's a laugh in itself . . .
Home late. Secretive phone calls. Leaving the room and
whisper, whisper. Have it out with him, she said. And I
should've done.

Steven   Why didn't you then?

Debbie   Because I was scared! I didn't want to . . . to lose . . .
I'm eight months pregnant, Steve. *Eight* months.

Steven   . . . I know.

Slight pause.

Debbie   Are you seeing Janis?

Steven   What?

Debbie   Are you fucking Janis?

Steven   No.

Debbie   Well, it's her you've been calling late at night. I checked your phone – Jesus! Don't lie to me!

Steven   I'm not lying.

Debbie   I phoned the office last week. They said you were out having lunch. I knew where you'd be. La Forchetta. Where you always go. You'd be sitting where you always sit. The single table by the window. You'd be cleaning your knife and fork with the serviette. Then you'd straighten the tablecloth and ask the waitress for a Diet Coke with ice and lemon. You'd spend ages looking at the menu and then order what you always order. *Escalope al limone* with side order of peas. Any garlic bread, sir? You'd think about it for a moment, frowning, then say what you always say. No. When the meal arrives you'll have black pepper but only on the veal please. You'll cut the meat into exactly the same-sized little bits. You won't look at the person sitting opposite you. Not once. You won't ask how their meal is. You won't tell them how yours is. When you've finished you'll move your empty plate to another table immediately and gaze out of the window. You'd ask for the desert menu but in the end you settle for a cappuccino. Then you'll go to the bathroom and clean your teeth with that little airport toothbrush you keep in your breast pocket. Then you'll suck a peppermint so strong it makes your eyes water. Then you come back to the table and pay with your credit card and leave a ten per cent tip worked out to the last bloody decimal point. Then you'll say, 'No rest for the wicked,' and rush back to the office. At some point on the way back you'll mention how you've eaten too much and should go to the gym and the

person you're with says, 'You look fine just as you are.' Like
I used to. Although now, of course, it ain't me. It's Janis.

Pause.

Steven   I'm seeing a ghost.

Debbie   What − ?

Steven   A ghost, Debbie. I'm seeing a ghost.

Debbie   What you fucking playing at now?

Steven   I've . . . I've seen it a few times.

Debbie   Jesus Christ. Chloe said you'll come out with some
bollocks.

Steven   It's not bollocks! Look at me! Does it . . . does it look
like I'm making it up?

Debbie   You look like my dad used to. When he came home
after from one of his sluts. Guilty.

Steven   Guilty?

Debbie   Yes. Guilty. Guilty and ashamed.

Slight pause.

Steven   A few weeks ago, on the way back from Barry's, I
stopped off at the supermarket. You asked me to get some bits.
Remember?

Slight pause.

Debbie?

Debbie   Go on. I'm intrigued.

Steven   It was late. The supermarket was practically empty.
I picked up the basket and walked down the aisle. I was tired.
I had a headache coming on. I thought, I'll get some aspirin or
something while I think of it. I turned into another aisle and −
There he was. The child.

Debbie   What child?

Steven   The boy. The boy I nearly knocked down. The same hair. Jeans. T-shirt. For a moment I couldn't move. I wanted to say something but . . . nothing. Then the kid walked away. I rushed to the end of the aisle. Gone. I looked down all the other aisles. Nothing. I ran around the supermarket time and time again like a fucking lunatic. The security guard came up to me. I asked, 'Have you seen a boy?' He said, 'No, sir. Have you lost your son?' I didn't know what to say. I just left.

Slight pause.

A few days later I was driving to work. It was early. The sun was coming up. Crisp and cold. I turned into Vallance Road and – there he was. Standing in the middle of the road. Exactly like before. I swerved the car to avoid him again. The car screeched to a halt. Some people stopped and stared. I got out of the car, I looked round at the people and when I looked back – the boy had gone. 'Did you see him? You must've seen him!' They hadn't. It was a ghost, Deb.

Slight pause.

I told Janis because I remember her telling me –

Debbie   Oh, here we go.

Steven   Her husband died of some blood-clot thing – aneurysm.

Debbie   Jesus.

Steven   She told me how she used to . . . to feel his presence in the flat where they lived. Sometimes Jan used to hear her husband's fingernails scraping the side of the armchair. Like he used to when he watched television. Jan went to this spiritualist meeting. At Hackney Town Hall. It's held the first Friday of every month. That's where I was last week.

Debbie   Jesus.

Steven   I hoped there would be a message for me. From this boy. There wasn't.

Debbie   Oh. Shame.

Slight pause.

Steven   Afterwards Janis introduced me to the medium.
I explained what had . . . what had been happening to me.
The medium asked me if I'd ever had any experiences like this
before. I said no. I said my brother had though.

Debbie   When?

Steven   After Dad died. Barry said he kept seeing him in the
shed at the back of our garden. Barry would spend all day in
the shed sometimes. Just waiting . . . waiting for Dad. Me and
Mum would find him sitting under Dad's desk with tears all
over his face. He wasn't scared.

Slight pause.

Debbie *goes to pick up rug.*

Steven   Deb! The medium explained this boy ghost probably
needs my help in some way. 'But why me?' I asked. 'And why
now?' The medium explained the 'now' part was probably due
to the car accident. Sometimes a trauma can . . . unlock things
inside you. That's what's happened to me, Deb. Something has
unlocked . . . opened me . . .

Slight pause.

Debbie *picks up rug and goes to leave.*

Steven   Deb! Tonight I . . . I couldn't sleep. I . . . I turned
the telly on. Kept the sound down. Some news report. Bombed
buildings. A screaming woman. Blood in the gutter. A shoe –
Then I saw it. The boy. He was standing there. Right behind
you.

Debbie   And you dropped the cranberry juice.

Slight pause.

Goes to leave again.

Steven   Please, Deb.

Reaches out for her.

Debbie   Fuck off!

Slight pause.

Steven   I don't want this to be happening to me.

Debbie   You don't?

Steven   Deb . . . I don't want Mum to know.

Debbie   What?

Steven   If Barry knows he'll blurt it out to her. Please keep this to yourself.

Debbie *walks out.*

Steven   Please, Deb! Don't tell Barry . . . Don't tell Barry . . .

12

Steven   'Ice!' Someone mentioned ice. I'm at the top of the stairs. Barry's next to me. He's crying and he's clutching the banisters – 'Frozen!' Something's been frozen. I peer between the banisters. The front door's open. Snow outside. People going in and out. Treading slush into the house. Down the hall. Into the living room. Mum won't like that. I can hear Mum crying. I can see shadows moving in the front room. Boots. Strange boots. I can hear walkie-talkies crackle. Police. I want to rush down but I know I mustn't. I've got to keep out of the way. The whole house feels different. It's two days since Dad went missing – 'Peaceful!' What's peaceful? I know all these words have something to do with Dad. Every time one of them is said Mum cries louder. Keep listening . . . Victoria Park . . . Canal . . . Dad has been found now. He's been found in the canal by Victoria Park. The canal has frozen over. Dad is in the ice. He looks peaceful.

13

Liz*'s new flat.*

Steven *and* **Liz**.

Steven *no longer has a walking stick.*

Liz   It's just that everything is so new. The houses, the street, the shops. It's like they've just been unpacked . . . Steven?

Steven   What – ? Oh, sorry, Mum.

Liz   You sure you're okay?

Steven   Yes, yes.

Liz   I would say I don't like the neighborhood. But you've got to have neighbours to have a neighbourhood. Don't see a soul. Don't hear a soul – Tell a lie! Heard a car door slam the other morning. No rubbish. No blobs of chewing gum on the pavement. There's nothing to . . . to remind me . . . of anything. It's all so polished and . . . There's no cracks to hold on to. I'm slipping off all the time. I should never have let you persuade me to leave the old place.

Steven   What?

Liz   On and on about the dog.

Steven   Me?

Liz   'I'll get you somewhere new. I'll pay the rent. You won't have to do a thing.'

Steven   I was trying to help, Mum.

Liz   'You'll never have any peace if you stay here.'

Steven   I never said that.

Liz   You did.

Steven   No. I didn't.

Liz   You . . . did.

Steven No!

Slight pause.

Mum . . . sit down. Please.

Liz What?

Steven I've got something to tell you.

Liz What's wrong?

Steven Nothing. I just . . . I just want to tell you something before you . . . before you hear it from someone else and you . . . you get the wrong end of the stick.

Liz You're making me nervous now.

Steven Sit down!

Liz *sits.*

Slight pause.

Steven Debbie thinks we've got rats.

Liz Rats?

Steven In the cellar.

Liz Your house is brand new.

Steven I know.

Liz They've only just finished building the other houses.

Steven Yes, yes.

Liz Have you seen their droppings?

Steven What?

Liz Rat shit? You seen it?

Steven No. I'm . . . well, I'm not sure.

Liz Droppings are the giveaway sign. You should put some bits of paper on the floor. With food on. And if the papers moved in the morning then you know you've –

Steven   Mum! Listen!

Slight pause.

Debbie don't want to risk staying in the house.

Liz   . . . Oh.

Steven   She's nervous about stuff like that. With the baby on the way.

Liz   . . . I see.

Steven   Infections.

Liz   Oh . . . yes.

Steven   So she's . . . she's gone to live with her sister for a while.

Liz   When?

Steven   . . . Last night.

Liz   I see.

Steven   Just till I get it sorted out. The rats. That's if we have rats. Which I don't think we have.

Liz   But she does?

Steven   . . . Yes.

Slight pause.

Liz   Well . . . you best sort it out quick then.

Steven   Yes, of course.

Liz   You don't want the mother of your child living somewhere else.

Steven   Of course not.

Liz   And I certainly don't want to schlep all the way to Debbie's sister's every time I want to see my grandchild. Not from here – Where's she live again?

Steven   New Cross.

Liz   Take me all bloody day.

Steven   It won't come to that.

Liz   I should hope not.

Slight pause.

Can you cope?

Steven   What?

Liz   The cooking? The cleaning?

Steven   I can look after myself, Mum.

Liz   I was still doing your washing till you met Debbie.

Steven   Mum. I can load a washing machine.

Slight pause.

Liz   I remember when I first saw Debbie. I paid you a surprise visit in the office. Remember that? I was on the way to the cinema down Mile End with Jerry.

Steven   Jerry?

Liz   From the decorating shop.

Steven   Oh.

Liz   Striking woman, I thought. Debbie. I knew there was something going on between you. You denied it. But you can't lie to me.

Steven   I didn't lie. There wasn't.

Liz   I'm your mother, Steve.

Steven   Debbie'd only been there a few days when you first saw her.

Liz   There was still something going on. At least from her. I thought, She's older. But that's no bad thing. I was older than your dad, bless him. About the same as you and Debbie.

Steven   It's only six years, Mum.

Liz Only? Tell that to Debbie. I remember looking at your dad when we were getting married. I thought, 'What am I doing? He's just out of his teens. He's still a little boy.'

Sound of bike pulling up.

Oh! That's your brother.

Steven You . . . you didn't tell me he was coming round.

Liz I didn't know. *He* don't make appointments.

Goes to door.

Barry (*off*) Hello, Mum.

Liz (*off*) Hello, luv.

Barry (*off*) Steve here?

Liz (*off*) Yes, yes.

Barry *enters.*

Barry Hello, brov.

Steven Hello.

Liz Do you wanna cup of tea, luv?

Barry Love one.

Liz Want another one, Steve?

Steven No.

Liz 'No thank you, Mum.'

Steven No thank you, Mum.

Liz *goes to kitchen.*

Slight pause.

Barry Debbie said you'd probably be here.

Steven Did she?

Barry I've been phoning you all morning.

Steven   Oh?

Barry   Debbie said she's left you.

Slight pause.

She said you hit her.

Slight pause.

Well?

Steven   I didn't.

Barry   She's got a lip out here, Steven.

Barry   She fell. In the cellar.

Barry   Oh, so that's it?

Steven   What's 'it'?

Barry   Chloe said you'd've worked some bullshit story out to tell me.

Steven   It's the truth.

Barry   So . . . what? She was going down to the cellar to . . . what? Look for something of Mum's? To check for rats?

Steven   I don't know why she fucking went down there.

Barry   She's over eight months pregnant, you cunt.

Liz *comes back with cup of tea.*

Liz   One tea, three sugars.

Barry   Thanks, Mum. Lovely.

Liz   I was just telling your brother what it's like to live round here.

Barry   I told him you wouldn't like it.

Liz   I don't.

Barry   Mum likes her things around her, I said.

Liz   Oh, I do.

Barry   She likes people to gossip to.

Liz   Oh, I do.

Barry   She'll miss her garden.

Liz   It always looked so lovely this time of year. Leaves like . . . like . . .

Barry   Sunset.

Liz   Oh, yes. The things I had to leave behind. My lovely wardrobe. Solid walnut. The dressing table too.

Steven   They were junk.

Liz   Steven.

Barry   They were antiques, brov.

Liz   They were.

Steven   Veneered chipboard.

Liz   What's he going on about?

Steven   House clearance wanted paying just to take the bloody crap away.

Barry   He's getting a bit wound up, I think, Mum. Violent, you could say.

Steven   Shut the fuck, Barry.

Liz   Don't talk to you brother like that.

Barry   That's the real Steven showing his colours.

Liz   What?

Barry   He told you about Debbie, Mum?

Liz   What – ? Oh. Yes. I don't blame her. Rats. Nasty.

Steven   I told Mum. Debbie thinks we've got rats. She's gone to live with Chloe till it gets sorted out.

Barry   Jesus! You believe that? Mum?

Liz   What, dear?

Barry   The rats?

Liz   Well, all houses can have rats.

Steven   Exactly.

Barry   His place ain't got rats. Unless it's him. Unless he's the bloody rat.

Liz   Now, now, don't call your brother names.

Barry   Why not? What would you call someone who hit their wife.

Liz   Hit their − ? I can't follow you sometimes.

Barry   I'll say it slowly then.

Steven   He's drunk.

Barry   You know I'm not.

Liz   We're so proud of you, Barry.

Barry   Mum! Listen to me . . . Your eldest son here hit his wife.

Steven   Don't listen to him.

Barry   In the face. Punched her. Last night. As a result she, quite rightly, has packed her bags and left him. Now, Mum, what bit of that didn't you follow?

Pause.

Liz   Drink your tea, dear.

Barry   Jesus.

Liz   Who wants biscuits?

Steven   Yes, please, Mum.

Liz   I've got some special ones.

Barry   Why do you always bloody believe him? Eh? Every fucking time.

Liz   Oh, the language.

Goes to kitchen.

Barry   Steve says it, so it must be true.

Steven   Why don't you just drop it?

Barry   Oh. Yes. That's the way it works in this family, ain't it? Believe what you wanna believe. Twist this. Ignore the other. That's how we fucking survive, ain't it?

Liz *returns with biscuits.*

Barry   Ain't it, Mum? Eh?

Steven   Don't listen, Mum.

Barry   You . . . you believe him cos he wraps all the painful stuff in feathers and flowers. Makes it all safe and cosy. You can't feel the broken glass inside.

Liz   He's making my head spin.

Steven   Mine too.

Barry   Remember when I did that drawing of Dad?

Steven   Shut it, Barry.

Liz   What's he going on about?

Barry   I did a drawing of Dad in the canal. At school. I spent ages on it. The teachers encouraged me. Said it was good for me. And it was. Fuck knows, I couldn't talk about it at home. The headmaster put it in the open-day exhibition. And what did you do, Mum? When you came to the open day and saw it. What did you do? Eh?

Liz   . . . It was a long time ago.

Barry   You tore it down.

Liz   I don't remember that.

Barry   You tore it down. Tore it into pieces. You shouted at the headmaster. You hit me, Mum. Remember that? Round the face.

Liz   I've never hit either of you boys. Have I, Steve?

Steven   No.

Liz   Not once.

Steven   Never.

Barry   My nose bled.

Steven   You imagined things.

Barry   The headmaster said if it wasn't for the pressure Mum'd been under he'd've called the police.

Liz   What pressure?

Barry   Dad's fucking suicide!

Long pause.

Liz   Biscuits?

Offers biscuit to **Steven**.

Steven   Thanks, Mum.

Liz *offers biscuit to* **Barry**.

Barry *shakes his head.*

Liz *takes a biscuit.*

Steven *and* **Liz** *eat.*

Pause.

Barry *dials on his mobile.*

Barry   Ask Debbie yourself, Mum.

Steven   Barry.

Barry   If you've got nothing to hide, what's the problem?

Liz   I really don't want to −

Barry (*into mobile*)   Deb, Mum wants a word.

Holds phone out.

Slight pause.

Steven   You don't have to do this, Mum.

Barry   Mum? Please.

Slight pause.

Liz *takes mobile.*

Liz   Hello, luv, how are you? . . . Fine, fine . . . Steven tells me you've got rats so you've gone to stay with –

Barry   Don't! Just . . . just ask her what happened.

Liz   I *am* asking.

Barry   You're not!

Snatches phone back.

(*Into mobile.*) Tell Mum why you left, Deb. The truth. Okay. Do it for me. For *me*.

Gives phone back to **Liz**.

Slight pause.

Liz (*into mobile*)   Can you hear all this, luv? I'm afraid to open my mouth in case I say something wrong at the moment. Anyway, we've got our orders . . . Tell me.

Pause.

Mmm . . . Yes . . . I see . . . No, no, of course I understand . . . Don't cry, luv, it'll all be fine. You'll see . . . Bye now, luv.

Hangs up. Gives phone back to **Barry**.

Barry   Well?

Slight pause.

Liz (*at* **Barry**)   How can you tell such lies?

14

Steven*'s house.*

Steven *and* **Liz**.

Steven   Why . . . why didn't you ring?

Liz   I did.

Looks round.

Don't tell me you've been eating takeaways?

Steven   When . . . when did you?

Liz   What?

Steven   Ring.

Liz   All bloody morning.

Steven   All – ? What's the time?

Liz   Two o'clock.

Steven   Jesus. Two? Two?

Liz   I rang the office. Couldn't get anything out of that Janis woman. I'm sure she's remedial. In the end I phoned Marky boy.

Steven   What did he say?

Liz   Enough to bring me here.

Picks up clothes.

Dirty?

Steven   Eh?

Liz   Washing machine.

Steven   Oh.

Liz *goes to kitchen.*

Liz   My God! When did you last do the washing-up?

Steven   I . . . I can't work the machine.

Liz   What's wrong with the sink and hot water?

Returns with refuse sack.

We used to clean houses before there were machines, you know.

Steven   How did you get here?

Liz   Bus.

Steven   Oh, Mum.

Liz   I've buried two parents and a husband, I'm more than capable of catching a bus

Starts picking up rubbish etc.

Steven   Don't.

Liz   It's not gonna clean itself.

Steven   I'll do it.

Liz   You're not well.

Steven   I'm fine.

Liz   You've got a fluey bug thing.

Steven   No, no.

Liz   Steven. You've got a fluey bug thing. Listen to Mum. You've got a fluey bug thing and Mum's here to help. Sit down. Sit down, Steven. You've got a fluey bug thing and you need to sit down. You need to do what Mum says and sit down. Now.

Slight pause.

Steven *sits.*

Liz   How long's this rubbish been hanging round? It's no good trying to get rid of the rats and then leaving food all over the place. You don't want Debbie coming back and seeing the place looking like this. She'll take one look and go straight

back to her sister's before you can say . . . oh, I dunno. Germ
warfare. And I wouldn't blame her. The baby's due in two
weeks, Steven. Two weeks.

Steven   I know.

Liz   Well, *look* like you know – Where shall I put this?

Steven   Over there.

Slight pause.

Liz   I said to Debbie, 'The rats must've gone by now, luv,'
I said. 'Rats don't last for ever.' She said, 'Yeah, Liz, I think
you're right.' I said to her, 'Of course I'm right,' I said. 'Why
don't you go back home where you belong?' She said, 'Oh,
Liz, it's difficult to talk about.' I said, 'Debbie,' I said, 'I'm
family and you can tell me anything. No secrets here.' She said,
'Well, Steve's been acting a bit . . . odd lately, Liz.' I said,
'Odd, luv. Can you explain it any more than that?' And she
said, 'No, Liz, I can't.' I said, 'Don't you worry about a thing,
Debbie, luv. I know exactly what's wrong with Steven. He's got
a touch of the fluey bug thing, that's all. I'll go round and see
him.' And here I am – There! That's a bit tidier now. Don't it
look better? . . . Don't it?

Steven   . . . Yes.

Liz   Course it does.

Takes bag outside.

Returns with duster.

Your dad used to have this fluey bug thing. He used to have it
so bad you could almost see the fluey bugs hovering in the air
all round him. If you got too close, you could feel yourself
catching it too. You could feel it infect your blood. Like being
sucked down a dark plughole – that's what it felt like. Scared
me, I don't mind telling you. I wouldn't let him in the house
when he had it. 'You can stay in your shed,' I told him. And
that's what he did. For weeks and weeks sometimes. I made a
little bed for him under his desk. Very cosy it was. Snug. I'd

leave trays of food outside the door for him. When he was
finished he'd put it back outside. Sometimes he left little notes
on the tray telling me he loved me. He didn't like to be looked
at when he got the fluey bug thing. He covered the shed
windows with sheets of newspaper – You probably don't
remember any of this. It happened when you were young.
You'd only just been born the first time. It happened again a
few years later when Barry came along. Then it sort of wore
off. Your dad built up his antibodies – There! Cleaner! You see
what Mum does? You're gonna need some help when the
baby's born. Debbie won't be able to cope. She's not the sort.
You know that. I could live here. In that spare room at the
back. That's a lovely room. Most of my stuff's in the cellar
anyway. We could all be one big family. Wouldn't that be
lovely?

Leaves room.

Returns with glass of water and some tablets.

Hands water and tablets to **Steven**.

Liz   Here.

Steven   What're these?

Liz   Aspirin.

Steven   I don't need aspirin.

Liz   Yes, you do.

Slight pause.

Steven *takes aspirin.*

Liz   When your dad was sure all his fluey bug thing had gone
he'd come out of the shed. I'd make him take all his clothes
off before I let him back into the house. I'd throw the lot away.
Then I'd run him a hot bath and pour some disinfectant into
it. Your dad would soak for ages. I'd shave him as he lay there.
Then I'd cook him a shepherd's pie for dinner – his favourite,
remember? – and we'd eat it on trays in front of the telly, just
like normal. Just like nothing had ever happened. We never

talked about the fluey bug thing once it was over. What was the
point? We all get under the weather now and again. Talking –
brooding – that don't do any good. You have to get over it.
You have to move on. Otherwise you might be sucked down
that plughole and never manage to claw your way back up.

Pause.

Give me the glass.

Slight pause.

Give me the glass.

Steven *gives her the glass.*

Liz *takes glass to kitchen.*

15

Steven's *house.*

Steven   What do you want? . . . What am I supposed to
do? . . . Don't look at me . . . Don't!

Slight pause.

Tell me what to do . . . if you told me what to do I would do
it . . . Why don't you say something . . . Please . . . Why don't
you . . . ? Speak! Please!

Slight pause.

It's just you and me now . . . Us . . . In the dark . . . You and
me . . . In the house . . . What am I supposed to – Say something!
Don't look! Speak!

Slight pause.

I remember . . . burnt bits of paper – Why am I telling you
this? No one else to tell . . . No one to listen . . . Burnt pages.
Found them in the tin drum. Pages from Dad's notebooks.
Burnt. Edges like black feathers. Crumbling feathers . . . I took
them up to my bedroom. I lay them on my bed. Careful.

Fragile. Dad's scribbles and doodles – Why tell you? You don't tell me anything. You don't tell me your secrets. Do you? Do you?

Slight pause.

Black-feather pages . . . Scorched pages . . . Scribble and – Words! I can . . . I can make out words . . . My name . . . Barry's name . . . Dad – he's . . . he's so afraid of us! . . . He looks at us and he's scared . . . There's a drawing of a black tree. What's that mean? . . . Burnt tree? . . . 'Die' . . . The word die . . . Dad looks at us . . . and he . . . afraid. Black tree. Burnt feathers. Die . . . Page crumbles to black snow . . . Mess! My mess now! My mess on my side of the ziggy-zaggy line. I'll clear it up, fuck you. Don't look at me like that.

Slight pause.

Feather black dust stain fingertips . . . Black prints on everything I touch . . . On bed . . . on wall . . . Get it clean! – I want everything polished and silver. I want to live in a place without fingerprints . . .

Slight pause.

I'm tired . . . Will you let me sleep? I can't sleep with you looking at me . . . I don't want to see you . . . I need to go somewhere dark. No light. Dig a hole . . . Deep, deep hole . . . In deep hole you see stars. That's what they say. Is it true? Don't want that . . . Don't want to dream . . . Want to be in dark without dreams . . . Like a shark in an ocean of ink . . . I don't want that dream again . . . Not trapped in ice. Not ice in my eyes . . . in my mouth . . . my lungs . . . Just dark. Please. Dreamless dark . . . dreamless dark . . .

16

The cellar.

Steven *is on the floor.*

Barry (*off*)   Steve?

Slight pause.

(*Off.*) Steve?

Steven *stirs.*

Barry (*off*)   Steven?

Steven   . . . Barry?

Barry (*off*)   Where are you?

Steven   Here!

Barry (*off*)   Where?

Steven   Here! Here!

Barry *appears.*

Barry   What the fuck you doing down here?

Steven   Safer.

Barry   Stinks like a brewery.

Steven   Sorry.

Barry   What's wrong with the light?

Steven   Took the bulb out.

Barry   Why, for fuck's sake?

Stumbles on something.

Jesus Christ, I can't see a fucking – Upstairs!

Steven   No!

Slight pause.

Barry   Steven. I've just driven all the way down from Birmingham. Okay? In the fucking rain. In the fucking cold. I'm not in the mood for playing silly buggers. So listen very carefully. Okay? . . . You listening?

Steven   Yes. Yes.

Barry   Debbie's in hospital.

Steven   Hospital?

Barry   The baby, for fuck's sake. Mum's been trying to get hold of you all day. Debbie too. In the end they rang me.

Steven   Why?

Barry   Fuck knows. Cos, I tell ya, I don't give a shit. But now I'm fucking here I'm gonna do what I've been asked to do so – Up! Come on! I'll make you a cup of coffee.

Grabs **Steven**.

Steven   No.

Barry   Steven!

Steven   No! No! No!

Pushes him off.

Barry   Have you gone fucking crazy? Have you?

Steven   Brov, I'm sorry but . . . but I can't go back up there. Please don't make me. I need to stay in the dark . . . Please, brov. Please. Don't make me . . . go up there . . . please . . .

Slight pause.

Barry *lights a cigarette lighter.*

Steven   No light.

He blows out lighter.

Barry   Stop it!

Slight pause.

He relights lighter.

Look at me, brov.

Slight pause.

Look at me.

Steven *looks at* **Barry**.

Barry   Brov . . . what's wrong?

Steven *blows out lighter.*

Steven   I can't see it in the dark.

Barry   See what?

Steven   The ghost.

Barry *lights lighter.*

Barry   There is no ghost.

Steven   There is.

Blows out lighter.

Barry   There ain't.

Lights lighter.

Steven   There is.

Blows out lighter.

Barry   There ain't.

Lights lighter.

Slight pause.

Steven *hides his face from light.*

Barry *sees candelabrum.*

Barry   Fuck me! Memories, eh?

Steven   Don't light it.

Barry   What?

Steven   It makes the shadows move. I don't like moving shadows. The ghost comes out of moving shadows.

Barry   Jesus Christ, Debbie said you'd talk this ghost bollocks.

Steven Don't, brov! Don't! Put it down.

Barry *doesn't move.*

Steven Put it down.

Slight pause.

Barry *puts candelabrum down.*

Slight pause.

Barry Steve . . . I don't know what's going on. To be honest, brov, I don't give a toss. You've got yourself into some kind of . . . state over something. My guess? Janis.

Steven Janis?

Barry Fucking another woman. Baby on the way – major head-fuck in anyone's books.

Steven No, no.

Barry That's what Debbie thinks all this is about.

Steven She's wrong.

Barry Chloe thinks so too.

Steven She's always hated me.

Barry No, she hasn't.

Steven You know I wouldn't cheat on Debbie, brov. You know.

Barry No. I don't. I don't know fuck all about you. I never have.

Slight pause.

You know . . . you know what you're like to me, Steve? The fucking Kennedy assassination. An enigma in a . . . a mystery in a whatsit. Or whatever the fucking phrase is. But – hey! – that's what family life is, I suppose, eh? Full of lies and deceit and spin . . . and mind-fucks. Each one of us is either sitting in the back of a car waiting for a bullet. Or sitting at a window

waiting to pull the trigger. Or loading a gun waiting to shoot
the man who pulled the trigger. The trick is – while all this . . .
this bloody madness is going on – to comment on how beautiful
Dallas looks in the sunshine. You get me?

Steven   . . . No.

Slight pause.

Barry   Listen. I promised your wife I'll get you to the hospital.
She wants to see you. She needs you. In the middle of
unimaginable fucking pain – whose name does she call? Yours!
Why? Another fucking mystery in a whatsit. So . . . Okay, I'll
do my brotherly duty. And then, brov, and then . . . I will fuck
off. Not just back to Birmingham. But as far as I can fucking
go. Australia. California. If I'm lucky enough to get my hands
on a fucking spaceship I'll warp-speed it to the other side of
the fucking universe. *That's* how far I want to go. And once . . .
once I've fucked off this far I'll never – never! – want to see
or hear anything from you ever again. Not you. Not Debbie.
Not Mum. I want to forget all about the bloody lot of you.
I want . . . I want my life up until now to seem like a . . . a
dream. And I will wake up from this dream. And I will be
who I was really meant to be be . . . Now get your act together.
No bullshit.

Heads upstairs.

Steven   Did Debbie tell you about the T-shirt?

Barry   Eh? What T-shirt?

Steven   The ghost. It was wearing a T-shirt with something
drawn on it.

Barry   What?

Steven   I thought Debbie might've mentioned it.

Barry   Steven.

Steven   Each one was a different colour.

Barry   What was drawn on the fucking T-shirts?

Steven   . . . Stars.

Pause.

Barry *walks up to* **Steven**.

Long pause.

Barry *hits* **Steven**.

Steven *falls.*

17

The cellar.

Barry *is holding the lit candelabrum.*

Steven *is hiding under a blanket on the floor.*

Long pause.

Barry   Dad's funeral.

Pause.

The service was just about to start when . . . when the man . . .
turned up – Can't fucking say it. Fuck! Fuck!

Pause.

The man – he talked to Mum at the entrance to the chapel.
I said to you, 'Who's that, brov?' You said . . . you said, 'Never
seen him before.'

Pause.

The man had thick grey hair. So grey it was almost white.
It was all sort of swept back. Tidy. He was so fucking pale.
He didn't look ill or anything. Just . . . like a ghost. I said, 'It's
Mr Ghost.' We laughed. The priest shot us a look. Remember?

Pause.

The man gave Mum a hug – you know? I think that was
the first time I'd ever seen Mum hugged. By another man,
I mean. Dad never hugged her. Dad never even kissed her. You
remember Dad kissing her?

Pause.

The man sat in the back row. Mum came and sat between us on the front row. She said, 'It's an old friend of your dad's. One of his teachers. He heard about your dad's accident and wanted to pay his respects.' I kept looking back at the man. You know what I remember the most? He was the only one crying. Apart from me, that is. I was crying and the man was crying. Mum didn't. Not once. Nor did you.

Steven　I did.

Barry　Not one fucking tear.

Steven *sits up.*

Pause.

Barry　After the funeral this man – he came up and spoke to us. You and me. We were standing a little way off from the grave. Mum was talking to some of her workmates. The man told us he used to teach Dad English. He said Dad was very good at writing. The man said he still has some poems written by Dad from when he was a boy. He asked if we wanted to see them. You didn't say anything. I said, 'Yes, please.' The man looked at you and said, 'Why don't you and your brother come round next Friday afternoon?' He told you his address a few times. He didn't write it down. He just kept saying it over and over again until you could say it back to him. The man said, 'Best not to tell your mum. Memories of your dad's childhood – they might upset her. We don't want to do that, do we, boys?' We both said we didn't want that. And then . . . then the man took you to one side. He put something in your hand and said, 'Treat yourself and your brother.' He'd given you some money. I didn't know how much. Later, you bought me . . . what was it, Steve? Remember what?

Steven　. . . No.

Barry　Chocolate.

Slight pause.

All that week you kept saying to me, 'Bet you can't wait to see Dad's poems, eh, brov?' On and on. I wasn't allowed to forget them for a second. 'Three days to Dad's poems.' 'Two days to Dad's poems.' 'Tomorrow you'll be seeing Dad's poems.' By the time the day arrived I was – Fuck! I was almost hysterical. Wasn't I, brov? I was practically begging you to take me to see the man. Oh, you played it so cool. You were busy. Had so much to do. But in the end . . . oh, you relented. We walked the whole way. And we took all the back streets. As if you didn't want anyone to see us. The man lived in this big house on the corner. There was a big tree in his front garden. I was so fucking excited. I felt sick with it. I kept tugging at your hand. You kept telling me to calm down. You rang the doorbell. The man opened the door. He was wearing a dressing gown. I whispered to you, 'Has he just got up?' We went into his living room. The curtains were pulled and I asked him why. He said, 'I have a very bad headache. They're called migraines.' I said, 'Mum gets those all the time.' The man said, 'Would you like something to drink?' We did. He got us some Cokes. We sat down and talked about Dad. He told us how good at English Dad was. He said, 'Your dad was destined to be a great poet.' And you said, 'But he wasn't.' And the man said, 'Not yet he wasn't. But he died so young. Just thirty-five.' We both giggled at the idea of thirty-five being young.

Slight pause.

The man said to me, 'Would you like so see your dad's poems now?' And I said, 'Yes.' And the man said, 'Come on then. They're upstairs.' And the man stood up. And I stood up. But you didn't. I said, 'Come on, brov. Dad's poems.' The man said, 'I don't think your brother's interested. Is that right, Steven?' And you nodded. I remember being really angry. I felt like hitting you. I said to the man, 'Forget him!' And the man held my hand. We went upstairs.

Slight pause.

When I came back down I was crying so much I couldn't catch my breath. The man said, 'You brother found it all a bit too

emotional, I think.' He got us some more Cokes. You were
sitting on the sofa. You wouldn't look at me. I wanted you to
look at me. But you wouldn't fucking look. You kept your eyes
fixed straight ahead. I said I wanted to go. You said we wouldn't
go till I stopped crying. And I knew . . . if I wanted to get
home, then I had to stop the tears somehow. So I drank the
Coke and I thought of other things. I thought of Dad and the
way he carried me on his shoulders. After a while I managed
to stop crying. I dried my face on my T-shirt. When I was
totally calm you said, 'Okay. Let's go. Mum will be wondering
where we've got to.' We all stood up. The man led us to the
door. Then a thought occurred to him and he said, 'Oh.
Steven.' And he took you to one side. Just like he did in the
cemetery. And he put money in your hand. Just like the cemetery.
Only this time I could see how much. And it wasn't pocket
money. It was notes. A lot of money. You put the money into
your back pocket. On the way home – again we walked – you
said I mustn't mention this to Mum. It will upset Mum. And
we didn't want to upset Mum, did we? You bought me
something on the way back. Chocolate. When we got home
I said, 'Do you want to see Dad's poem that the man gave
me?' You said you did. I took a folded sheet of paper out of
my back jeans pocket. I remember it was damp with my sweat.
You sat on the edge of your bed and you opened it. And you
studied the piece of paper like you were reading something.
Only you weren't reading something, were you, Steve? You
weren't reading anything cos the paper was blank.

Steven   No.

Barry   There was nothing on it.

Steven   Dad's handwriting.

Barry   That's bollocks.

Steven   I saw it.

Barry   We didn't talk about the man for the rest of the week.

Steven   We did.

Barry   No. Not until next Friday when you said to me, 'I bet you want another one of Dad's poems, don't you?' I said, 'Please don't take me back there, brov. Don't take me to Mr Ghost.'

Steven   No.

Barry   You hit me.

Steven   No.

Barry   I fell to the floor.

Steven   No. No.

Barry   We walked the whole way again.

Steven   It was a two-fucking-bus journey. It wasn't worth the trouble. We both agreed that.

Barry   We took all the back streets like before.

Steven   I worked out a short cut.

Barry   I felt sick with fear.

Steven   With excitement.

Barry   I kept tugging at your hand.

Steven   Excitement.

Barry   I wanted to get away.

Steven   You couldn't wait to fucking get there.

Barry   Bollocks.

Steven   You were pulling my arm.

Barry   You were pulling me.

Steven   You were pulling me.

Barry   You rang the doorbell.

Steven   Yes.

Barry   The man opened the door.

Steven   Yes.

Barry   He was wearing a dressing gown.

Steven   No. One of those . . . old-fashioned smoking jackets.

Barry   No.

Steven   Yes. He liked that stuff.

Barry   I whispered to you, 'Has he just got up?'

Steven   'No, brov, it's a smoking jacket.'

Barry   We went into his living room.

Steven   Yes.

Barry   The curtains were pulled and I asked him why.

Steven   A little bit pulled.

Barry   Completely pulled.

Steven   No. No.

Barry   He said, 'I have a very bad headache. They're called migraines.'

Steven   Yes.

Barry   I said, 'Mum gets those all the time.'

Steven   Not all the time.

Barry   All the time. Every day. The man said to me, 'Would you like so see your dad's poems now?'

Steven   It was only the one poem.

Barry   Jesus, Steven.

Steven   It was one. It was.

Barry   It wasn't.

Steven   It was.

Barry   The man said, 'Come on then. They're upstairs.' And the man stood up. And I stood up. But you . . . you didn't stand up.

Steven   That's right.

Barry   I said, 'Come on, brov. Dad's poems.' The man said, 'I don't think your brother's interested. Is that right, Steven?' And you nodded.

Steven   I was there for you.

Barry   For *me*?

Steven   It was important you had these memories of Dad all to yourself.

Barry   To *myself*.

Steven   To help you talk about Dad.

Barry   I never stopped talking about Dad.

Steven   No. You hadn't mentioned him once.

Barry   No. It was you and Mum who never fucking mentioned him.

Steven   You hadn't cried.

Barry   I never stopped.

Steven   It was all . . . inside you. Locked up.

Barry   Locked up?

Steven   Everyone knew it. Mum was so worried.

Barry   Bollocks!

Steven *stands.*

Steven   I was worried.

Barry   Why you doing this?

Steven   Cos it's the truth.

Barry   No.

Steven   Yes. We didn't know what to do. And then – yes, that's it! This man came to the funeral. Old schoolteacher of Dad's. He talked to you about Dad. He said he had a poem

Dad wrote when Dad was about your age. I asked a teacher at school if it would help you to meet this man and talk to him about Dad's childhood – You see how it's all coming back now?

Barry   Stop it.

Steven   And the teacher said it would help. The teacher asked me to – No, the teacher *told* me to take you there.

Barry   No.

Steven   So we went to see this man. The first time we went the man gave you the poem Dad had written. You cried a bit but . . . oh, you were so much better after that.

Barry   You fucking bastard.

Steven   Shut up, Barry. Listen. It was like all the grief was leaving you. Everyone noticed the difference. Mum. Your teachers. I took you back to see the man for a few weeks after that.

Barry   It was . . . months. Months!

Steven   No! No! You soon got fed up with going. The man was sad not to see you of course.

Barry   Bastard!

Steven   But the man understood. He was glad to've been of help. He sent Christmas cards for a few years. Addressed to all of us. We sent cards back. Sometimes we enclosed a little photo we thought he might like. That one where you're wearing the T-shirt you drew stars on. Each one a different colour. Remember that? Mum got in a bit of a state. But even she had to admit it was well done. It was. I wouldn't mind a shirt like that now. You could mass-produce them, brov. I'd help set you up. Sell them down Camden Market or somewhere. Appeal to you? Why don't we do that, brov. You interested?

Slight pause.

Perhaps not.

Starts looking for something.

What happened to the man in the end? Do you know, brov?

Slight pause.

He died, I think. Recently, I think. We were invited to the funeral but we were all so busy. Babies. Alcoholism. Car crashes. These things get in the way, don't they? They shouldn't. They do – Here it is!

Finds light bulb.

There was a photo of Chloe in the local newspaper the other day. You see it? Janis pointed it out to me. Just after I fucked her – Only joking!

Screws in light bulb.

Snow White. That's what Chloe's in. Pantomine down at Stratford. She's Snow White. I would have thought the Wicked Queen was more her type, the fucking bitch – Only joking. Have you fucked Chloe, brov? Debbie said you did. Or you wanted to. Or Chloe wanted to. You fucked Janis, didn't you, brov? Marky boy said you did. Or did he say you fucked him? Or wanted to? Fuck me, the possibilities. Endless.

Turns light on.

There! . . . Blow the candles out, brov.

Barry *doesn't move.*

Steven   Blow the candles out, brov.

Barry *doesn't move.*

Steven   Blow the candles out, brov.

Barry *starts blowing the candles out.*

Steven   She was in a crystal coffin. Chloe. In the photo. Underneath it said: 'Snow White awaits the kiss that will bring her back to life.' We should go and see it. Shall we do that, brov? All of us. Big family night out. Me, you, Mum, Chloe, Debbie. That's if the birth goes okay. It could be a stillborn or something. Very common, I hear – Oh! You can put the candelabrum down now, brov.

Barry *doesn't move.*

Steven   You can put the candelabrum down now, brov.

Barry *puts the candelabrum down.*

Steven   Not there.

Slight pause.

Barry *moves candelabrum.*

Steven   Not there. Jesus, brov. Don't you know where candelabrums go? They go here.

Moves candelabrum.

That's the place for candelabrums. Can you remember that in future, please? Brov! I've just thought. If the baby is born alive and survives . . . You'll be an uncle. Uncle Barry. How does that feel? Uncle Barry. Uncle Barry. I know, I know, bit of a shock. You know what I think you need, brov? A drink.

18

Steven*'s house.*

Steven *and* **Liz**.

Debbie *(off)*
  Twinkle, twinkle, little star,
  How I wonder what you are . . . *etc.*

Liz   Listen to her.

Steven   She's a natural.

Liz   Who would've thought it?

Slight pause.

The baby alarm works a treat.

Steven Yes.

Liz Told you I'd find something else to buy.

Steven It's perfect.

Liz I think the cot you bought is a bit . . . big.

Steven It is a bit.

Liz You don't mind me saying.

Steven You can say what you like, Mum. You know that.

Liz Baby looks lost in it.

Steven Debbie's choice.

Debbie *enters.*

Debbie Fast asleep.

Steven Good.

Liz I said to Steven, 'The baby alarm works a treat.'

Steven I said, 'It's perfect.'

Debbie Yes.

Slight pause.

More tea, Liz?

Liz No, no, I'm fine.

Debbie Steve?

Steven No.

Slight pause.

Liz It's so peaceful here, ain't it?

Steven Double glazing.

Liz You need it these days.

Steven You do.

His mobile rings.

Answers it.

Yes? . . . No, no, the contract from last May . . . Yes – Eh? No, I can't phone them now . . . I don't care . . . Well, tell him I've just got back from my brother's bloody funeral and I'm sorry but I'm a bit tied up . . . Look, I've got to go . . . Thanks, Steph.

Hangs up.

Slight pause.

Liz   Is that the baby?

They listen.

Pause.

Steven   No.

Liz   No.

Debbie   No.

Slight pause.

Liz   Your brother was so looking forward to the baby. Your brother would have taught him all about art. Painting. He was gonna be a famous painter. Barry. He was just . . . finding his feet. Wasn't he, Steve?

Steven   He was, Mum.

Liz   You remember that exhibition he had? When he was a student. That was a lovely night, wasn't it?

Steven   It was.

Liz   And Barry's paintings – oh, they were the best. I couldn't stop looking at them. The colours. Relaxing. I wanted them for my living room. You remember that, Steve?

Steven   That's right.

Liz   But someone bought them.

Steven   You were so upset.

Liz   I was. I cried, I think.

Steven   You did.

Liz   I thought I did.

Slight pause.

Is that the baby?

They listen.

Pause.

Steven   No.

Liz   No.

Debbie   No.

Slight pause.

Liz *starts to cry.*

Steven   Oh, Mum. Don't – Get her a drink.

Debbie *goes to cocktail cabinet.*

Debbie   . . . What?

Steven   A sherry, for fuck's sake.

Debbie *pours sherry.*

Steven   Come on, come on.

Debbie *gives sherry to* **Steven**.

Debbie   Is she okay?

Steven   Sit down.

Debbie *sits.*

Steven *gives sherry to* **Liz**.

Liz *sips.*

Slight pause.

Liz   I knew he should never have bought that motorbike.
I had a bad feeling about it. I said to you. Didn't I, Steve?
I said.

Steven   Yes, Mum.

Liz   He had an exhibition coming up. Everything was just
falling into place for him. He was going to be a famous painter.

Steven   He was, Mum.

Liz   I've lost both parents, a husband and a son. Ain't I
suffered enough? Eh? Ain't I suffered enough?

Steven   Oh, Mum. Please. Don't.

Holds **Liz**.

Pause.

Liz   You . . . you've always looked after me, Steve. Always.
Remember after Dad's accident? Those months?

Steven   Yes, yes.

Liz   That was a . . . a strange time, wasn't it? Hard to
remember much now.

Steven   I know.

Liz   I went down with a touch of that fluey bug thing, didn't I?
Oh, it was awful. All I wanted to do was sleep. I couldn't
move. You had to do all the housework. Cooking. And every
week . . . you bought me a present. You remember that, Steve?

Steven   . . . Yes.

Liz   A little ornament. Glass – He knew I loved glass. I
remember – oh, my favourite thing! He bought me this glass
tree. Big thing it was. Wouldn't fit on top of the telly. I put it in
the middle of the dining table. Remember that?

Steven   Oh, yes.

Liz   Beautiful it looked. Had all these branches and twigs.
Sparkled in the light. And then . . . every week . . . You bought

me a beautiful glass leaf to hang off the branches. The smaller twigs were shaped like hooks and you . . . hooked them on. Remember? The leaves were so . . . so detailed. They had veins and they were all swirling with colour. Every week . . . for months . . . a leaf . . . until the tree – oh, the tree was this shimmering . . . tinkling . . . Must've cost you a fortune. Don't know where you got the money. But . . . oh, I'm so glad you did. Because . . . it saved me. Truly. Saved me . . . Whenever I think of . . . of those months . . . I think of glass leaves . . .

Pause.

Is that the baby?

Steven   No.

Liz   No.

Debbie   No.

Steven   And then . . . then this gust of wind came along – real strong – and . . . and Dad – he grabs hold of my hand. So sudden. So tight. His nails dig in. I try to pull away but Dad just holds tighter and tighter. I look at him. The scar by his left eye is sort of twitching. Like it does when Mum's shouting at him and he don't say a single word back. I say, 'Dad . . . you're hurting me!' But still he won't let go. I can see he's holding Barry's hand just as hard. Barry's face is all screwed up. Again I say, 'Dad! You're hurting me.' Again his grip gets tighter. It's as if . . . as if Dad's afraid the gust of wind is going to blow him away . . . and we'll lose him for ever.

Baby's cry, off.

Blackout.